FAMOUS IN *heaven* & AT *home*

A 31-DAY CHARACTER STUDY OF THE PROVERBS 31 WOMAN

By Michelle Myers

Edited by Dr. Katie McCoy
Cover Art & Design by Stephanie Cantrell

“Inspiring and convicting, *Famous in Heaven & At Home* cuts through the noisy distractions of cultural expectations and calls women to live with a Kingdom-minded focus. Whether you’re a single college student, or career-minded woman, or a stay-at-home mom, this 31-day devotional will help you refocus your perspective, reorder your priorities, and renew your sense of purpose. Embarking on this journey with Michelle is like having your own spiritual life-coach. She’s fun and fearless, challenging and encouraging, solidly biblical and deeply practical. Famous in Heaven and at Home is a must for any woman who wants to honor God with a faithful heart and a well-prioritized life.”

Dr. Katie McCoy
Professor, Southwestern Baptist Theological Seminary

“It takes a wise, creative, and humble woman to tackle Proverbs 31 and not leave her readers feeling inadequate or discouraged. Michelle Myers does that with wisdom, grace, love, and gentleness. This is a journey worth going on with her. And this is absolutely a journey worth going on with the Lord. Let's not be scared of God's Word, but trust His loving and gracious heart towards us.”

Jess Connolly
Author, Wild & Free and Co-Founder of Naptime Diaries & The Influence Network

“The fastest way to influence and serve others is by example, and that requires living according to our values and priorities. Using Proverbs 31 as the foundation, Michelle breaks it down with a practical approach that simplifies the steps we must follow to live a life that honors God and our families first. Michelle is a humble teacher. Her style is real, fresh, relatable and refreshing. Michelle helps us understand how our lives are simplified and enriched when we put God at the center of all things.”

Chalene Johnson
NYT Best-Selling Author and Founder of the Smart Success Academy

"Our culture is begging for someone to strike the balance for women to be both feminine and fierce, care givers and catalytic leaders, beautiful and bold. Michelle Myers has done it in *Famous in Heaven & At Home*. This book provides inspiration and the practical steps to empower and unleash women to fulfill God's intended purpose for their lives. Michelle is straight-forward, funny and most importantly, leads by example for today's generation of women to follow."

Andy Savage
Teaching Pastor, Highpoint Church (Memphis, TN)

"I've been hearing about this Proverbs 31 woman for 15 years but Michelle has revived this passage for me! Her approach is fresh, straightforward, Biblical and practical for everyday life and each day I am left motivated and hopeful for a new day to live for Jesus in the extraordinary moments and just as much in the mundane!"

Valerie Woerner
Author of The Finishing School and Owner of Val Marie Paper

"The book sparks a beautiful reflection of what God's plan and purpose is for women. Michelle is inviting, captivating, and relevant. I can see why the title of this book is *Famous in Heaven & At Home*, as it encourages the reader to pursue God's calling in order to bring Him glory."

Katie Farrell
Dashing Dish

FAMOUS IN HEAVEN AND AT HOME
A 31 Day Character Study of the Proverbs 31 Woman

ISBN 978-0-9964009-2-3

contents

This book is dedicated to every woman out there chasing after Christ as hard as she can. I'm honored to work for His Kingdom alongside you, and I'm cheering you on. I value what you do for His mission.

Famous in Heaven and at Home. Let's do this. If we don't meet before we hit Heaven, I'll see you there.

before you read

When God first laid on my heart to write a character study of the P31 woman, I was full of objections.

My objections took many forms, but they all boiled down to one thing:

I'm not qualified.

So before you begin to dig in, please know my heart. Know that this is not an attempt to pretend like I have this mastered or have it all together. I'm coming to you, shaking in His strength.

But I am also basking in the truth that His Word will not return void *(Isaiah 55:11).*

That His power is made perfect in weakness *(2 Corinthians 12:9).*

And none of my insecurities matter when obedience is on the line.

My prayer is that the words here will provide to a deep Biblical study of this woman – the P31 woman – that will give us character goals rooted straight from the authority of His Word and encouragement to equip us, instead of just adding a set of requirements to our already full to-do lists. I pray this study will pour purpose over us as we pursue living life His way, and practical application into us as we put into practice the truths we are learning together.

Here's a brief highlight of the five sections that each day's devotional contains:

#P31Goal

Praise the Lord that He does not expect perfection from His children! But part of a growing relationship with the Lord is working to become more like His Son. Each day, we'll begin with a character goal we see embodied in the P31 woman.

#P31Authority

Just so we all know these were not goals created out of thin air, but rooted in God's instruction, this section will provide the exact wording from Scripture that puts God's stamp of authority on the day's goal that we are working toward.

#P31Encouragement

While these pages are going to be filled with truth from God's Word, the furthest thing from my mind is having anyone read a devotion that leaves them feeling beat up and defeated. Convicted? Maybe. The realization we've got some work to do? I know I certainly do. But my prayer is that the truth of His Word will breathe new life and purpose into us that we've perhaps never tapped into before. I want us to walk away encouraged to live in deeper fullness of Christ!

#P31Prayer

I love that you've picked up this book! But I will be honest... Instead of you holding a device in your hand, I wish you were holding a warm cup of coffee, and we were face-to-face. While I can't make that possible, I can pray for you, which is one of the greatest gifts and privileges He has allowed us to give one another. I may not know your situation, but He does. So as much as I'd love to buy you that cup of coffee and hear your story, I'm content to lift you up to our Father each day that we have together and trust that He is working in your life.

#P31Practice

We'll only impact our homes and take more to heaven with us if we put into practice what God is stirring in our hearts. We don't want anything to stay in our heads or hearts, but to extend to those God puts within our reach. Each day, we'll be challenged to put that day's truth into motion in our lives and let God provide the ripple effect to those around us.

day one

#P31Goal

Proverbs 31 is a character description of the woman God has called me to be, not a to-do list.

#P31Authority

The original Hebrew text shows Proverbs 31:10-31 as an acrostic poem of the Hebrew alphabet. Down to the intentionality of the literary form, we are drawn to see the big picture amidst the details.

#P31Encouragement

Be honest – there's a part of you that has always secretly despised the Proverbs 31 woman. I mean, I'd like to meet the woman who reads that chapter and thinks to herself, "Nailed it. Next assignment, God!"

I know I spent years reading this passage and would immediately feel inadequate and overwhelmed. *Is this even possible?!*

But as God has shaped my heart over the years, He has also helped me to see that this passage is not a job description where I must meet each exact requirement. If we take this passage literally, we wouldn't ever sleep! (Which, for the moms, I know we don't get much, but we still get some!)

If we look at the headings in Scripture (randomly dispersed between passages to help us identify key truths and central themes), you'll find descriptors like this:

NASB – "Description of a Worthy Woman"
ESV – "The Woman Who Fears the Lord"
NIV/NLT – "The Wife of Noble Character"
NKJV – "The Virtuous Wife"

See? Each of these headings references her character, her virtues, what defines her worth, and Who she lives for. It's big picture.

That's not all. Visual learners, prepare to have your mind blown!

Proverbs 31 is an acrostic poem that uses all 22 characters in the Hebrew alphabet (the original language in which the Old Testament was written.)

First of all, using the entire alphabet shows completeness, from start to finish. It's a visual that points to the big picture, the overall fullness of what we are to take away from this woman.

And we all know that life constantly brings change. But despite circumstances, character can remain consistent.

Plus, from a practical standpoint, acrostics typically aid in memorization. *(For example, if you were raised in my generation, I can guarantee that you use a certain acrostic for remembering the planets in their order from the sun. Thank you, Saved by the Bell.)*

This was not a poem to be read in one season of life one time. This was an oracle (more on that tomorrow) that we were intended to read, learn, meditate on, memorize, and live out.

10 :הרכמ םינינפמ קחרו אצמי ימ ליח-תשא

11 :רסחי אל ללשו הלעב בל הב חטב

12 :היחי ימי לכ ער-אלו בוט והתלמג

13 :היפכ ץפחב שעתו םיתשפו רמצ השרד

14 :המחל איבת קחרממ רחוס תוינאכ התיה

15 :היתרענל קחו התיבל ףרט ןתתו הליל דועב םקתו

16 :םרכ העטנ היפכ ירפמ והחקתו הדש הממז

17 :היתעורז ץמאתו הינתמ זועב הרגח

18 :הרנ הלילב הבכי-אל הרחס בוט-יכ המעט

19 :ךלפ וכמת היפכו רושיכב החלש הידי

20 :ןויבאל החלש הידיו ינעל השרפ הפכ

21 :םינש שבל התיב-לכ יכ גלשמ התיבל אריִת-אל

22 :השובל ןמגראו שש הל-התשע םידברמ

23 :ץרא-ינקז-םע ותבשב הלעב םירעשב עדונ

24 :ינענכל הנתנ רוגחו רכמתו התשע ןידס

25 :ןורחא םויל קחשתו השובל רדהו-זע

26 :הנושל-לע דסח-תרותו המכחב החתפ היפ

27 :לכאת אל תולצע םחלו התיב תוכילה היפוצ

28 :הללהיו הלעב הורשאיו הינב ומק

29 :הנלכ-לע תילע תאו ליח ושע תונב תובר

30 :ללהתת איה הוהי-תארי השא יפיה לבהו ןחה רקש

31 :היׂשעמ םירעשב והוללהיו הידי ירפמ הל-ונת

So we can take a deep breath. Our role in life may not look the same. Our season of life may look different. But despite role or season, our character can mirror this woman's.

Let's set the record straight: Above all, Proverbs 31 is a character description we are all capable to implement.

Over the next 31 days, I am inviting you to lay down your to-do lists. To lay down your personal agenda. To pray against "checklist Christianity."

Let's dig deep into this woman's character and see what God wants us to put on display to a world that so desperately needs to see Him.

#P31Prayer

God, we thank you so much for the above-and-beyond measures You take to reveal Yourself and Your message in Your Word. We praise You for how intentional You are in Your pursuit of us, despite how undeserving we are of Your love and Your grace. God, I ask that we would lay down any preconceived notions about this passage. I pray that each day as we approach the text that it would be as if we were reading it for the very first time. I pray that we would fight against our natural tendencies to throw up our hands in defeat, but that we would open our hearts to what You have to say. Show us where we can improve. Give us the same focus for intentionality in pursuing this noble character as You have shown for our hearts. We humbly admit that we cannot do this huge task on our own. We need You. Come show Your infinite power in our lives. Do this work in us and through us. We love you. Amen.

#P31Practice

It's so tempting to approach God's Word selfishly. To say, "God, show me something I can use in my life." While there's certainly plenty of room for application from the Bible, let's think bigger this month. Let's refuse to limit ourselves to simply application.

The **#P31Practice** is going to give you plenty of application on what to take away and begin implementing. But I would love to invite you to journal each day with what this particular passage reveals to you about God's character. If it's something He asks us to do, how has He already displayed this in Himself and who He is? If we are made in His image, the things He will ask us to reflect will easily be evident in His character, too. Let's not miss what this rich passage reveals to us about Him as we learn what He's calling us to reflect in our lives.

What can I learn about God's character from today's reading?

day two

#P31Goal

P31 comes to us God-breathed from the heart of a woman.

#P31Authority

*The sayings of King Lemuel – **an oracle his mother taught him.***
Proverbs 31:1

#P31Encouragement

That's right. This passage was not written by a man. The verdict is still out as to whether Pinterest is a conspiracy created by a group of men who are tricking women everywhere into cooking, cleaning and working out...but we don't have to wonder with Proverbs 31.

It comes straight to our hearts, woman to woman, from King Lemuel's mother. God stitches being a woman of His standard onto our hearts, but it's consistent with the teaching throughout His Word that we would receive this passage from Godly woman.

Titus 2:3-5 says, "Older women, likewise, are to be reverent in behavior, not slanderers or slaves to much wine. They are to teach what is good, and so train the young women to love their husbands and children, to be self-controlled, pure, working at home, kind, and submissive to their own husbands, that the word of God may not be reviled."

So many prickly words to this world in just a few verses. Working at home. Submissive. It's no doubt many women would find offense in this passage.

But it's only if we have allowed ourselves to be influenced by our culture more than our Creator that we find this offensive. This is not a restriction of what we can do; this is instruction of what He has *called* us to do.

Let's get real; we're not very good at this. Even within our churches and Kingdom work circles, I see far more competition, cattiness and comparison than I see women seeking to affirm, bless, and instruct one another to grow closer to the Lord.

It grieves my heart.

While there are many reasons for this trend, I just wonder if we've gotten distracted. Though we may not be doing something necessarily "bad," by our omission of living this out, we're neglecting a key instruction to women in God's Word. Yet instead of dealing with our disobedience, we're tempted to grasp at inferior reasons as to why women aren't making more of a ripple effect in the Kingdom.

It's easy to assume that our ineffectiveness is because we should have "his role." That believing "his role" would give us more of a voice or more influence. But maybe it's just because we haven't taken our role – *our critically important role* – seriously enough.

Before you think you're not an "older woman" yet, that description is not just referring to age; it's referencing spiritual maturity. So even if you are a brand new believer, there are still women out there who don't know Jesus yet, and you can be an "older woman" in their life.

Get even more practical: If there's a woman you follow, or a woman chasing after Jesus at the same pace as you, I can make you one promise: you can never encourage her enough. In fact, the harder she is chasing after Christ and the bolder she is in living for Him, the louder the shouts of the enemy. Your encouragement to her is more than words; it drowns out Satan's lies.

Plus, many add to the text here. By saying "workers at home," it doesn't mean you can't work outside of your home. In our study of the P31 woman, we're going to see quickly there's quite a bit she does outside of the walls of her home.

But her home is not neglected in the process. She's more than physically present in her home. She's actively working to serve her family well.

I help run three businesses/ministries. My husband is a pastor. We have a lot of responsibility outside of our home. We also have two boys, and a little girl on the way. The majority of days, despite the day's professional demands, the hardest work I do all day is inside my home.

Don't get me wrong. It's by far the most rewarding work, and the blessings outweigh the hardship. But the demands of running a home are challenging: physically, spiritually, mentally, emotionally challenging.

I don't think any of us would argue that being a wife and mom isn't worthy work. Let's take that conviction and also recognize we can't fulfill these roles well if we aren't willing to put in the required effort.

Why am I spending all of this time in Titus 2? Isn't this a study in Proverbs 31? Yes, but seeing how the Old Testament and New Testament weave together matters. The New Testament doesn't make the Old Testament irrelevant. It makes the Old Testament make sense. The same things we see emphasized in Titus 2 are the very same topics we are going to expand on in Proverbs 31.

The truths we're going to dig into are timeless. They were true for King Lemuel's mother. They were true 2,000 years ago in New Testament times, and they still ring true for us today.

In a world that is constantly changing, aren't you grateful for a God who is the same yesterday, today and forever?

#P31Prayer

God, we thank you that you've never changed, not even once. In an ever-shifting world, we are grateful for the firm foundation that is You. God, help us to see beyond ourselves and see Your big picture. Give us glimpses of Your perspective. Your ways are higher than our ways, and Your thoughts are higher than our thoughts. There's no possible way to even comprehend the wisdom You have. So even in the things we may not understand, help us prioritize Your wisdom over our earthly ignorance. Help us to see all the freedoms and roles You've given us to pursue, and help us to chase after those with passion. Help us to take Your instruction to us seriously. Guard us against our own flippant arrogance. You are God, and we are not. Thank you for allowing us to participate in Your agenda. You don't need us, but You choose to use us, and we are so grateful. We love you. Amen.

#P31Practice

We live in a world that's quick to criticize and slow to encourage. Would you make the decision now to be an encourager? To take seriously the instruction to teach "younger women" in your life by your word and example?

Avoiding comparison and competitiveness among women is something taught inside and outside of Christian circles. But the reason the topic continuously arises is because it's still rare to see it lived out. Let's stand in the gap. Let's be the answer. When comparison is discussed, wouldn't it be awesome if Christian women became the simple solution instead of continuing to contribute to the problem?

Pray for her. Smile. Breathe life into others. Give hugs. Go out of your way to say something kind. Write encouragement notes. Make phone calls. Partner together. Promote others. Step out of the spotlight, and shine His light on someone else.

That's something our world will notice.

If you want to join in, She Works His Way started **#buildherUP** as a way of kicking comparison in the teeth on social media. We'd love for you to join in!

What do I need to allow God to work on my heart in with regard to comparison?

____

____

____

____

Am I more frequently quick to encourage or quick to criticize?

____

____

____

____

____

What are ways I can go out of my way to encourage others He has placed in my life?

day three

#P31Goal

I am more concerned with knowing God than being known.

#P31Authority

A capable wife, who can find? For her worth is far above jewels.
Proverbs 31:10

#P31Encouragement

You've got to love a great rhetorical question. What this verse implies is that a man on his own power cannot find such a woman. She is more than just capable (more on that in a minute), but she is rare.

One of my personal heroes, Elisabeth Elliott, put it this way:

"A woman's heart should be so hidden in Christ that only a man seeking the Lord can find it."

So, we hide our hearts in the Lord. A man seeks the Lord. Then, God brings the two together in His perfect timing and His perfect way.

This isn't just a one-time thing. His love is the only love that is perfect. So whether we're still waiting on God to bring a spouse into our lives or we've been married for decades, the fact remains: His love is the only reliable glue for our marriages, and it's an every day choice. We must bask in His love first to be able to give it away ourselves.

This requires that we have to ask the question: "What is God looking for?" His Word gives us two great answers:

> *The Lord does not see what man sees. The man looks at the outward appearance, but God looks at the heart.* 1 Samuel 16:7

> *Rather it should be that of your inner self, the unfading beauty of a gentle and quiet spirit, which is of great worth in God's sight.* 1 Peter 3:4

God is looking at the condition of our hearts. Our actions matter, but God is examining even the motives behind our actions.

In the Hebrew, the word "capable" refers to her ability, her efficiency, her wealth, her endurance, her energy, her valor, and her virtue. So "capable" refers to much more beyond mere competence.

It puts her in a category that reflects Christ more than herself.

We live in a world where everyone is trying to make a name for themselves. Everyone is looking to be accepted, and unfortunately, we spend too much time dwelling in all the wrong places.

Let me give you a sweet, gentle reminder: You do not have to fight for your acceptance. He has already accepted you. Do not fall victim for the world's lies that you have to fight for your worth. If you have accepted Jesus as your personal Lord and Savior, God has already deemed you worthy.

If we rely on Facebook likes and Instagram hearts to determine our worth, we're settling for the instant gratification that comes from opinions that largely don't matter. We're also ignoring the only approval that has authority – God's.

There's nothing wrong with having a platform, especially one that is rooted in ministry. But it's the heart behind the platform that matters. If we're aiming for having the character of the P31 woman, being known by others can't be our priority. Knowing God and helping others know God must remain our ultimate goal.

So what happens when we ask the question, "Am I more concerned with being known or knowing God?"

What gets our time, thought, and effort? Trying to blaze our own trail, seeking to prove our worth as we go, is going to prove to be both meaningless and exhausting. On the other hand, when God knows us, He is going to fill in our gaps, direct our paths, and lead us where He wants us to go.

It's not ultimately about finding a man. It's about recognizing that knowing God intimately and living our lives loudly before Him is the key to unlocking the rare worth He has planned for us.

Wouldn't it be tragic if we missed it?

#P31Prayer

God, don't let us miss the opportunity to find our worth in You. This world offers us so many cheap knock-offs to Your divine plan. Open our eyes to detect the counterfeit offers. Don't let us waste our time succeeding at things that don't matter. It can't be about us, Lord, but it has to be about You. We are finite; You are infinite. We are created; You are Creator. God, I pray that You give us opportunities to be bold ambassadors for You, but keep us in check. If we become filled with pride or selfish ambition, I pray You would strip every opportunity away until we get right with You. Fill us with the attitude of Jesus – that we would always hold Your agenda and priority over our own and that we would consider others before ourselves. We want to make You famous,

Lord. Hold our hearts there, and don't let them move from Your precious presence. We love you so much. Thank You for loving us first. Amen.

#P31Practice

Andy Stanley once tweeted, "If God did everything you were asking Him to do in your life through someone else, would you praise Him just the same?" Let's force ourselves to ask that question. Talk about a serious gut check.

To recap: God delivers the results we're praying for. The outcome is the same. The only thing different is that He chose to use someone else to accomplish it instead of us.

If we would have a hard time praising God in that situation, we have just exposed seeds of selfish ambition in our lives. There is tangible evidence that we struggle with the desire to be known.

Let's be active in cutting that sin off today. Craig Groeshel wrote, "Celebration delivers a kill shot straight to the heart of envy." Think of someone you admire, someone who is walking a path that you hope God takes you down someday. Instead of admiring them from afar, or maybe even harboring a little jealousy in your heart of how God is using them over you right now, take some time to encourage them today. Whether you know them personally or it's just someone you can reach out to on social media, send them some encouragement. Celebrate them and what God is doing through them. Let the kill shot ring!

If God did everything I was asking Him to do in my life through someone else, would I praise Him just the same?

____

____

____

____

____

____

____

____

Who can I encourage today, and what will I do?

____

____

____

____

____

day four

#P31Goal

I am my husband's safe place + an asset to his life.

#P31Authority

The heart of her husband ***trusts in her****, and he will have* ***no lack of gain.*** Proverbs 31:11

#P31Encouragement

Our heart is the innermost part of us. Proverbs 4:23 goes as far to refer to the heart as the "wellspring of life."

Let's think practically: our husbands see us at our worst, and we see them at their worst. There's a reason why traditional marriage vows include the "for better or for worse" clause!

We mustn't breeze over these words without considering their weight. What does it mean if the person we see at their worst has a heart that safely trusts in us?

For our husband, I think this covers three areas; It means he can always trust our intentions, our confidentiality and our affections.

• ***Intentions***

Marriages that have more suspicion than trust are in trouble. My pastor, Bruce Frank, once said a hilarious but true statement, "If Jesus had to die to save your spouse, there's a good chance they may do a few things that get on your nerves."

Here's the reality: we made an unconditional commitment to an imperfect person. So did our husbands. We can expect conflict to arise. It's how we approach and handle that conflict that matters.

We must first resolve to be on the side of our marriage. When conflict occurs, it can't be about us vs. him. It has to be about both of us choosing to stand on the side of our marriage and reach a conclusion that ultimately strengthens our relationship.

This takes work. This takes knowing ourselves and knowing our spouses. But if we will do the extra work required, remain on the side of our marriage, and give our husbands enough evidence to know that (even when we disagree) we love them and value them, the effort is always worth it.

• ***Confidentiality***

Can our husbands share something with us without worrying that we might share it with their best friend or our mother? Do they feel like they have a "man card" to protect, or can they be completely vulnerable with us?

If they can, his heart can safely trust us. If we've betrayed that trust, or shared things he shared with us in confidence with those who don't need that information, it will limit emotional intimacy in our marriages.

Intimacy grows in small spaces. The more things that are shared between just the two of you will only strengthen the cords of your relationship. The more things that are withheld from one another will only drive a wedge. Go the extra mile to strengthen the relationship and avoid anything that creates distance.

• ***Affections***

Of course, we must address the obvious. Your husband needs to know you think he is the sexiest man alive. Contrary to the belief that Christian marriages are boring, the opposite is true. Relationships with the deepest levels of trust and intimacy allow the most freedom and pleasure.

If our husbands feel like we don't desire them or they are fighting another man for our affections, we are not protecting his heart. No, this doesn't give him permission to act on his hurt, but we must realize that our actions can help protect him against temptation.

Obviously, that's the extreme. But what about the simple? What other things might they feel are competing for our affections?

> *Are we so consumed with motherhood that we've stopped prioritizing being his wife?*
>
> *Or are we sitting in the same room with him, staring at our phone or the TV, wrongly convinced that we are spending "quality time" together?*
>
> *Does our job, or even our calling, get more of our energy than he does?*

Let's make sure that our husbands undoubtedly know of our undying affections for him. In the greatest marriages, the "honeymoon" phase isn't the sweetest season of marriage. It's just the start of the greatest seasons of life. Each season of life should show increased intimacy, affection and love for one another.

Secondly, "he will have no lack of gain" means that we are an asset to our husbands. We increase his credibility. When people meet us, they should simultaneously think more of our husbands.

Of course, this boils down to our personal integrity and our character. Embracing a character that overflows with kindness and joy in hand with grace and humility is a winning combination to ensure that who we are is to put us in a position to propel our husbands forward rather than holding them back.

#P31Prayer

God, thank you so much for the gift of our husbands, whether we're currently doing life with him or we're still waiting for him to come into our lives. Help us to see him as a gift to our lives from You. Guide us to live intentionally in a way that pursues his heart and allow him to trust us completely. Rid my heart of an attitude of unnecessary suspicion and criticism toward him. Close my lips against sharing things with others that should remain just between us. Make my actions prove to him that I am his safest place on this earth. Give me the energy and attention to put my affections for him on display. Give me the desire to love him how he receives love the most clearly. Help who I am only increase who he is. Mold my character to be more like You so that I can be the best asset to him possible. Thank you for being the foundation of our marriage. We love you! Amen.

#P31Practice

Meditate on these Casting Crown lyrics from "Slow Fade:"

> It's a slow fade when you give yourself away.
> It's a slow fade when black and white have turned to gray.
> Thoughts invade, choices are made, a price will be paid,
> When you give yourself away.
> People never crumble in a day.
> Daddies never crumble in a day.
> Families never crumble in a day.
> ***It's a slow fade.***

Are there any "slow fades" in your marriage? Bottom line: the less intentional we are in our pursuit of one another, the less intimacy and joy we will find within our marriages. The majority of marriage issues could be solved with greater pursuit of one another.

Protect your marriage against that slow fade by making sure your husband gets a priority, reoccurring slot on your intentional to-do list. What's something you can do every day to show Him that your intentions, your confidentiality and your affections are an asset to him? Brainstorm on your man's needs, put your ideas into action, and bask in the joy of a growing, thriving, God-honoring marriage.

Here's a small idea: Each day, ask him the question, "Is there anything I can do to help you today?" He may not have an answer for you daily, but simply asking the question increases your involvement in his life and shows him you take being his wife seriously.

Are there any "slow fades" in your marriage? Write them down, and make a game plan of how to eliminate them.

____

____

____

____

How will I work to make my husband feel valued by me?

#P31Goal

My husband gets my best all the days of my life.

#P31Authority

She ***does him good*** *and not evil,* ***all the days of her life.*** Proverbs 31:12

#P31Encouragement

Let's just cut to the heart: It's easy to coast in neutral.

We were born with a sin nature, so it's probably easier for us to lean toward evil than to have a disposition toward good. But actually being intentional to pursue what is good requires work and effort.

We cannot actually do someone good if we are choosing to coast in neutral. Doing good means that we are making the choice to minister to someone else. In this verse, that someone else is our husband.

Very similar to the slow fade we referenced yesterday, we must remember that we only drift in one direction.

In its simplest form, we must remember that doing our husbands good means that we make him a priority in our lives.

We must aim so that our husband gets our best, not our leftovers.

Let me be the first to admit that this is hard – no matter what your life's season has for you right now, whether you think about a draining career or you're deep in the trenches of parenting. Maybe you're even juggling both of those plus more simultaneously!

The temptation is to coast in neutral, even if it's not evil. We arrive home from the day, maybe we have a bit of family time amidst ball practice, dinner, and homework, we finally get the kids to bed, and we want to do the Braveheart tribal "FREEEEEEEEE-DOM!" yell.

We are done. We want to check out.

Here's the question we must ask ourselves: Is this the exception, or is this the rule?

Because if we have given so much in every other area of our lives that we never have anything left to give our husbands, we've arranged our lives so that he's not making our priority list. A checked-out, worn-out wife can't bring her husband good if she has nothing left for him.

Maybe there's something that needs to come off your plate so that your husband gets a place back on your plate. Maybe you need to communicate better with one another so your schedules don't require that you miss one another so much.

Whatever the change needs to be, if we find our husbands are consistently just getting what we have left over, something needs to change.

Single ladies, I hope you haven't checked out on me yet, because I have seriously the coolest takeaway for you. Did you catch that the end of verse 12 reads, *"all the days of her life?"*

That's right. This truth does not just apply to all the days we are married. I'm pretty sure "*all the days of her life*" actually refers to ***all the days of her life***. This is so critical to remember in seasons of singleness and seasons of dating:

Am I doing my husband good before he is even in the picture?

Don't miss this: Becoming a woman worthy of the title of Proverbs 31 character does not mean that we are changing who we are to find a husband. It means we are cultivating who God has called us to be so that we are ready for him when we meet him and begin our lives together.

One of my mentors, Thomas White, shared this analogy with me when I was dating my husband. He said, "When you're single, you chase after God as fast as you can. While you're running, glance to your left and right, and see who's chasing God at the same pace you are. When you consistently see the same face over and over again, you grab hands and decide to chase after God together."

Doing him good is a result of that chase. Yes, we are pursuing the heart of our husbands. But we'll do the man God has given us the most good when we remain consistent in our chase of Christ, and one day, continuing that chase while refusing to let go of our husband's hand.

#P31Prayer

God, protect us against complacency. Don't allow us spend time drifting in neutral. We know that strong marriages require our consistent effort. Rearrange our priorities so that our hearts and our actions reflect Your order. Help us chase after You as hard and as fast as we possibly can. If we're married, help us to hold tightly to our husband's hand in the process of our pursuit of You. Give us a heart that desires for him to get our best, not our leftovers. If we're single, help us to practice our diligence and intentionality of an intimate relationship in our personal walk with You. Give us patience until You bring that man chasing after You at the same pace into our lives. Ease our loneliness with Your presence.

Whether we are married or single, help us to realize that You alone are enough for us. We love You, and we trust You. Amen.

#P31Practice

- ***For the married ladies:***

Lack of communication tends to be a backbone issue for many couples. Yes, the conflict may arise in different ways, but taking the time to communicate clearer with one another is often the best way to take out multiple problems at the same time.

Take some time to think about the areas where conflict typically arises in your marriage. Then, ask yourself, "Are there any of these conflicts that can be avoided in the future if we simply communicate better?"

I know it seems "unromantic" to think about developing systems in your marriage, but systems also are indicators of intentionality. One system that has drastically changed our marriage is realizing that, because both of us having ministry-related job, we often don't keep the typical 9-5 schedule. "After hours" hours are a reality for both of us.

What was killing us and the time we had to spend together was when we would fail to communicate to one another ahead of time about when those "after hours" would be. For example, James might be planning on a date night in after we put the boys to bed, not knowing that I had a She Works His Way webcast that evening. He ends up feeling hurt and neglected because of my lack of communication.

Now, we look months ahead and weeks ahead, and we share a calendar. When I look at the calendar, I can either plan my webcast for an evening when he is already scheduled for something so we are both working on the same night, or we can make sure that we sneak a date night or date day somewhere else into our week.

Work with your husband to create a more effective system for communication. Make it fun with dessert or candlelight. It doesn't have to feel like a business meeting. It's the two of you coming to brainstorm how you can make your marriage even better.

And that's exciting.

Brainstorm for Better Communication System in My Marriage:

____

____

____

____

____

____

____

____

____

____

____

• ***All the single ladies:***

Write your husband a letter. Express your love for him. How you can't wait to meet him. What you're doing in your life to bring him good. How God is sustaining you, but how you heart aches to meet him. Put him on your regular prayer schedule if he's not there already.

My husband and I began praying for each other when we were 11 and 13, respectively. Ironically enough, we're two years apart in age, so we began praying for each other during the same year. I knew I was going to marry him the first time we ever spoke, and if you know me, you know that I'm not an impulsive person. I can't state this as fact, but I can't help but believe that I was able to recognize him so quickly is because I had been praying for him for over a decade when we met.

If you're reading this, please know that I've prayed for you in this waiting season. I can't wait to see how God writes your love story!

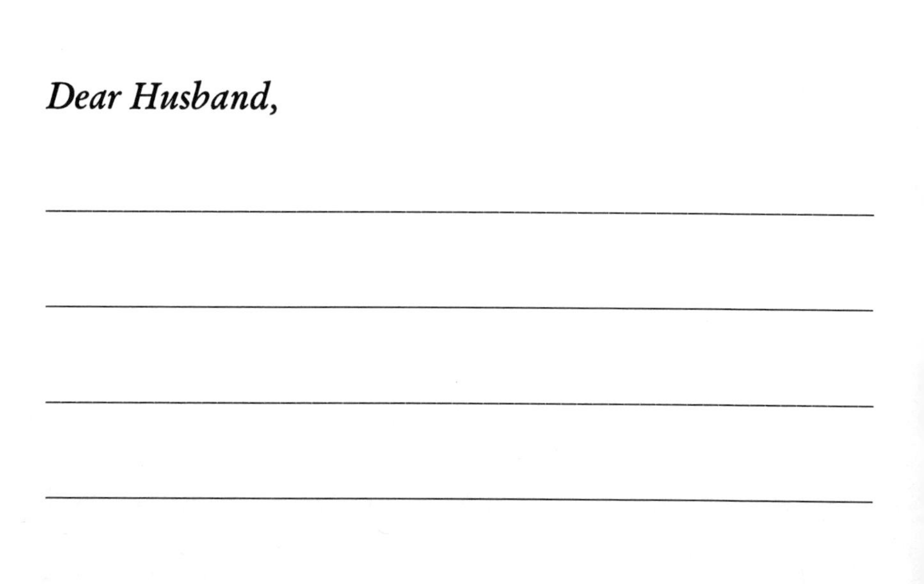

Dear Husband,

Love,
Your wife who loves you already

day six

#P31Goal

Caring for my family is a delight, not a duty.

#P31Authority

She looks for wool and flax, and ***works with her hands in delight.*** Proverbs 31:13

#P31Encouragement

For those of you who may be as domestically challenged as I am, let me shed some light. Wool and flax were two key ingredients for meeting basic household needs during the time this was written. Today, this might say, "She does laundry and fights long lines at the grocery store dangerously close to her toddler's naptime."

What matters is that we take away from this is that she prioritizes meeting the needs of her household.

But it's really the second part of this verse that matters even more. It's not really about her actions as much as it is about her attitude in completing the actions.

She works with her hands in delight. More than a duty, serving her family is a delight.

Let's just ask the question: "What's my attitude like when I'm required to do mundane tasks?"

Maybe you're in a season at home with young kids, and a large portion of your day consists of changing diapers, cooking and cleaning. Maybe you've got teenagers, and you feel like your day looks very similar to a taxi driver.

Do you delight in those things? If not, that's an attitude adjustment that can be fixed...again, with a little dose of intentionality.

For example, my mom used to pray for us while she folded laundry. Sometimes, we could even hear her. I'd peek around the corner, seeing her folding a pair of my socks, and I'd hear her praying for me. If I remember it all these years later, I know I was impressed then, but now that I'm in a similar season, I'm in awe.

It wasn't something my mom did for show. No one was around, and I'm sure she didn't think I was listening or paying attention. She was just serving her family out of the overflow of her character: a woman who had chosen a delight over duty mindset.

Confession: I do not do this perfectly...especially when I am folding socks. I am tempted to complain about that black hole that exists somewhere in my dryer that magically grabs one sock from a pair at a time. But since God convicted me about this in my spirit, when I catch myself beginning to complain, I choose to pray instead. I pray God will help me take the initiative to make the task a delight instead of waiting on myself to find a passion for folding socks. (That's never going to happen!)

When I change my attitude to mirror my mom's and the one we see exemplified in this passage, I can find magic in the mundane. Delight is there for me, but I must be the one to pursue it.

Let me take a second to talk to my moms who delegate. Maybe you've outsourced laundry, and you're wondering if I think you can't be a Proverbs 31 woman because you don't fold your family's socks.

That could not be further from my heart. Remember what we learned together on Day 1. This is a character description, not a job description.

But no matter how much you delegate, there will still be things in every household that fall back on you, and it's your attitude in those moments and tasks that matters here. This is about prioritizing being a willing worker and letting our household know that it is a delight, not a drag, to serve them.

Think about the service industry. Can't you immediately spot the worker who despises their job? On the flip side, isn't it easy to spot the employee who is joyful regardless of their circumstance or task? Doesn't the disgruntled worker almost put you in a bad mood, whereas the joyful worker inspires you effortlessly?

Let's do the same for our families. Let's inspire them to see mundane moments as opportunities for joy.

Remember this: duty is easy, but delight takes effort. Let's pursue the extra effort required to make the mundane magical.

#P31Prayer

God, we're quickly seeing that being a woman of this kind of character is no small task. There's no way that we can do it in our own strength. We need Your power and the attitude displayed in Jesus in order to make these qualities realities in our own lives. We do not expect perfection from ourselves, and we are grateful for Your grace that is there when we fail. But God, we pray that we would see tremendous growth in our hearts and lives with each day. We pray we would be able to look back and see evidence of joy and delight among tasks that used to be burdens and pointless. Show us areas where we have opportunities for joy. Give us Your eyes to see things that we would miss on our own. Go before us. Use us as an example of what a joyful and humble servant looks like to those inside our homes. Correct us when our attitudes are less than this instructs, give us the humility to apologize to those we displayed poor attitudes to, and give us an opportunity again to show a character that reflects You to our families quickly. Thank you for Your power that works for us, in us, and through us. We love you so much. Amen.

#P31Practice

What's the most mundane task you do in this season of your life? Make a game plan for finding joy in that task. For some accountability, we encourage you to tell someone close to you about your revised plan, and ask them to hold you accountable by regularly asking you if you are serving with delight there. Repeat this exercise often. It's worth it!

How will I find joy in the most mundane tasks in my life? (Come back here, and repeat this exercise often!)

____

____

____

____

____

day seven

#P31Goal

I prioritize my "for sure, for sure" callings from God over every other opportunity.

#P31Authority

*She is like merchant ships; **she brings her food from afar.*** Proverbs 31:14

#P31Encouragement

Did you ever think you would be compared to a merchant ship? When we allow ourselves to pull back the lens and grasp the big picture, we see this instruction is much bigger than food.

This analogy forces us to wrestle with the question, "Am I willing to do whatever it takes to ensure my family is well provided for?"

Career mamas, I know you know something about providing. But this is not just referring to money. Since we're here, let me offer a small caveat that I feel is relevant to share.

The moment our career or our income becomes more about building our name, our fame, or our platform, we've encountered dangerous ground. We've allowed ourselves to stumble into selfish ambition, and if there's anything I would be willing to go out on a limb and say God can't use, it's a heart that seeks its own fame more than His glory.

If we see seeds of that in our own lives, we've given Satan a foothold, and we need to leap back as quickly as we can into the arms of our Father. If we are going to remain Kingdom-effective, our hearts must stay pure, and our priorities must honor Him before ourselves.

So when it comes to making sure our families are well provided for, let's think about the title God gave me for this book. Let's seek to be famous at home first. We can trust God with the when's, how's, and the what's of our influence outside of our home.

But let's not belittle the influence He has given us inside our homes. There is fertile soil there that we are unquestionably called to fertilize and nurture.

What do I mean by "unquestionably called to"? We each have callings on our lives that we never have reason to doubt because there are certain assignments God has given to no one else.

No one else can handle your walk with Christ.
No one else can be the wife to your husband.
No one else can be the mother to your children.

There are "maybe callings" where we can allow God to open doors for us and walk through in obedience to Him. But even as God turns those maybe callings into clear direction, our "for sure, for sure" callings – the assignments He has given to no one else – do not go away, and the priority of their importance does not change.

Remember the promise in Luke 16:10, "Whoever can be trusted

with very little can also be trusted with much, and whoever is dishonest with very little will also be dishonest with much."

If God can't trust us in the assignments that He has graciously granted to us alone, why would He have reason to give us more?

#P31Prayer

God, please help us never to take for granted the assignments that You have given only to us. I know even before I was married with children, I struggled with giving You my whole heart. I fought selfish ambition of wanting more than just You. Then, I got married, and I again fought for my timing in starting a family. Then, I had children, and I still find myself constantly needing to remind myself of my assignments that matter most. No matter what season I've been in, I've struggled to pursue my highest callings – the tasks that You have given to no one else but me. Forgive us when our hearts betray the trust You've entrusted to us with those assignments. Lead us to a place that longs to make You famous and to be famous within the walls of our homes here on earth. We trust You to grant us more opportunities if we prove ourselves trustworthy in these "for sure, for sure" callings You've graciously given us. If there's anything in our lives that seeks our own fame over Your glory, we pray that You would strip it from us for the sake of Your eternal Kingdom that matters so much more than our fleeting existence. We desperately need You at work in us. Remind us of this truth daily. We love you. Amen.

#P31Practice

Is your heart pure in your work? Are your motives where they need to be? Are you living your life in those "for sure, for sure" callings in this season of your life in such a way that He can give you more?

Today, I encourage you to write God a letter of adoration for who He is and confession of what you need to do better in the assignments He has given to no one else.

Then, get alone in a quiet place with a sheet of paper. On the left column, write down any seeds of selfish ambition you feel in your heart, even if they are just sprouts. On the right column, look up and list specific Scripture verses that combat why those selfish thoughts are not of God. *(If you're unsure of where to start, I'd recommend Philippians 2 and Romans 12 as great passages to read.)*

Slowly, start working through the list of Scriptures you write down, and commit them to memory. As you feel selfish ambition start to flow out of your heart, you will be armed with the same weapon in your mind that Jesus used to crush Satan in Matthew 4: God's mighty Word.

Is my heart pure in my work? How so, or what will I commit to work on?

____

____

____

____

____

____

Does the way I pursue my "for sure, for sure" callings show God He can trust me with more?

My Letter to God:

Selfish Ambition Seeds	*What Scripture Says is True*

day eight

#P31Goal

I am willing to do whatever it takes to accomplish whatever God has called me to do.

#P31Authority

*She **rises also while it is still night** and gives food to her household and portions to her maidens.* Proverbs 31:15

#P31Encouragement

Confession: I do not love getting up early...but I am blessed with early risers. So if I am going to be able to have any "me time" to pray, read my Bible, exercise, etc., it has to happen earlier than I prefer.

But again, this is not a job description. It does not mean if your alarm is not set for 5am that you are ineligible to be a P31 woman.

What this verse teaches us about her character is that we must have a "whatever it takes" attitude.

Am I willing to do whatever it takes to accomplish whatever God has called me to do?

Having a wiling heart won't happen by accident. Think about it: we are born selfish, and for our entire lives; we fight against pursuing our own desires.

Trading *selfishness* for *selflessness* is one of the rarely given and most precious gifts we can give those around us. It's also one of the most obvious ways to embody the attitude of Jesus and put the gospel on display.

Just think about Philippians 2:3-4: "Do nothing out of selfish ambition or vain conceit. Rather, in humility, value others above yourselves, not looking to your own interests but each of you to the interests of others."

The passage goes on to describe how Jesus, though He was God, didn't even consider equality with God something to be grasped (vs. 6), and that He "made Himself nothing" (vs. 7), and humbled himself to the point of obedience in His on a cross (vs. 8.)

Because of this, *"God has highly exalted Him and bestowed on Him the name that is above every other name"* (Philippians 2:9).

The same promise is true for us. Every time we choose to pursue what is best for God's glory, what is best for others, we set ourselves up to be lifted up by God.

Luke 14:11 reminds us, *"For all those who exalt themselves will be humbled, and those who humble themselves will be exalted."*

Now, let's not make sure we don't get it twisted. These blessings from God are not promised to occur here on earth. As James 4:14 so bluntly puts it, *"What is your life? For you are a mist that appears for a little time and then vanishes."*

But if eternity with Jesus in heaven is the only blessing we ever receive from God, we've still out-punted our coverage.

Maybe it's not a 5am wake-up call that displays your "whatever it takes" attitude. Maybe you've put your professional career on hold to stay at home with your young kids. Maybe you stay up until 2am so you can have time with your husband when he gets home from the night shift. Maybe you've built a business from scratch that you diligently pursue at naptime. Maybe it has been years since you've slept the entire night through.

I may not ever know the sacrifices you've made, and many others may never be aware either. But none of that matters, because God sees it all. Hebrews 4:13 reminds us that "*nothing in creation is hidden from God's sight.*"

Our "whatever it takes" is never wasted. We serve a God who longs to be gracious to us *(Isaiah 30:18)*. His Word assures us that honor follows humility *(Proverbs 29:23; 22:4)*; that humility is proof that we are walking in His wisdom *(James 3:13)*; that humility brings healing *(2 Chronicles 7:14)*, and that the greatest freedom exists for us as we humbly serve others in love *(Galatians 5:13)*.

#P31Prayer

God, we admit that it's difficult to serve others humbly. We selfishly fight our desire to hear appreciation and praise. But Father, regardless of whether we hear it audibly from others or not, help us to spend time at Your feet so we can feel Your approval of our sacrifices. Help us to be disciplined to do "whatever it takes," but also give us the humility to do it willingly. Sustain us as only You can. Send doses of encouragement when we need it most. But above all else, Lord, we beg You to show up in our lives. A "whatever it takes" attitude is not a one-and-done event, but a daily occurrence. Help us to experience Your glory in the grind. Thank you for caring for us so deeply. We love you. Amen.

#P31Practice

Jon Bloom highlighted seven "D's" to pray over our hearts for a "whatever it takes" attitude on Desiring God.[1] Bloom writes, "'Whatever it takes' prayers help me press toward and express childlike trust in the Father."

The seven D's he suggested to pray over are:

- Delight
- Desires
- Dependence
- Discernment
- Desperation
- Discipline
- Diligence

Because there are seven, I've worked these traits into my daily prayers for my myself and the hearts of my family. I highly recommend you read his entire blog post, dive into the Scriptures listed, and spend the next week watching your heart transform through the power of prayer. God hears us, He is not silent, and prayer is such a productive use of our time.

For those of you with elementary age children, I also suggest utilizing Ted Tripp's concept of having your kids begin a "heart journal." You can read more about this in his *Shepherding a Child's Heart: Parent's Handbook.* Bottom line: our kids are never too young to learn their behaviors are an overflow of their hearts. If we address their behavior and miss the opportunity for heart training, we are setting them up for rules-based obedience instead of relationship-based obedience, not just to us, but to God.

[1] www.desiringgod.org/articles/seven-ways-to-pray-for-your-heart

Prayer Journal for a "Whatever It Takes" Attitude

Prayer over my Delight:

Prayer over my Desires:

Prayer over my Dependence:

Prayer over my Discernment:

Prayer over my Desperation:

Prayer over my Discipline:

Prayer over my Diligence:

day nine

#P31Goal

I will faithfully serve those God has called me to lead.

#P31Authority

She rises also while it is still night and ***gives food to her household and portions to her maidens.*** Proverbs 31:15

#P31Encouragement

Bottom line: We cannot represent the character of a P31 woman if we are unwilling to serve. Before we dig into having the heart of a servant, let's note the two groups she is actively serving: her family and those she is leading.

When she gets up, providing for her family is the first thing on her mind. She is thinking ahead for their needs. They get her priority-energy.

Let's be honest: there are so many things that compete for your time. Not all of them are bad, but we are doing ourselves a disservice if we don't recognize that we will always have an opportunity to be distracted from the things that matter most.

For example, let's chat about the Facebook newsfeed. Is it really necessary to scroll through it mindlessly 17 times per day? (Before you dismiss that as an exaggeration, Facebook's 2015 earning report showed that the average user spends 46 minutes per day, and 65% of users are active daily on Facebook.[2])

I'm not telling you to delete your Facebook account. But I am telling you that if you find yourself staring at your phone while your husband or kids are trying to talk to you, there's a problem.

"Giving food to her household" isn't simply the act of making sure they have something to eat for their breakfast. It's ensuring that, above any other activity we are involved in, providing for our family's needs remains our top responsibility – not just in what we say, but in what we actually do.

Rachel Macy Stafford put it this way, "What if you missed hearing the best part of your child's day because you were on the phone? What if you missed a chance to inhale the sweet scent of your energetic child because you insisted on folding that basket of laundry before bedtime? What if you missed a chance to console your worried spouse because of your mile-long to-do list?"[3]

We won't always get it right, but if we make conscious efforts to give them our priority-energy, we should ensure we'll get it right more than we'll get it wrong.

Now, let's chat about those "maidens." This implies that she's not trying to do everything alone. She has others working alongside her. If there's a common problem among women today, I believe that most women think that everyone's doing a better job than they are and they are desperately trying to "do it all."

For example, in today's world, I think most women believe

---

[2] www.investor.fb.com/releasedetail.cfm?ReleaseID=924562

[3] Stafford, Rachel Macy. *Hands Free Mama: A Guide to Putting Down the phone, Burning the To-Do List, and Letting Go of Perfection to Grasp What Really Matters*

that it, in order to be considered a "put together women," they must have successful husbands with thriving, date-night-filled marriages; well-behaved children who excel both at school and sports; a blossoming career that comes so naturally, it's effortless; a Pinterest-worthy home; a wardrobe that both looks designer and costs them nothing (only to cover their toned body as a result of their daily workouts and drool-worthy kale smoothies); and of course, shampoo commercial-worthy hair, and wrinkle-free, sun-kissed skin. All wrapped up with a carefree smile that belongs on a toothpaste ad!

But that life does not exist.

Effortless results do not happen. And God gave each of us unique gifts so we would function better together. We were purposefully created to need one another's gifts *(1 Corinthians 12).*

We were created for companionship and teamwork, not to do life alone.

The word "maidens" may bring up confusion, since some would assume this means the P31 woman hires people to do everything for her. But this very verse negates that idea completely. The first time we're introduced to the people she is leading and delegating responsibility to, she isn't being waited on.

She is actively serving them.

True leadership is being a servant. We are never leading more like Jesus than when we are serving others. In fact, the best leaders do more following than leading.

Paul wrote, "Follow me as I follow Christ" *(1 Corinthians 11:1).*

That's the kind of leadership we see on display in Proverbs 31. It's one that says, "Get in line behind me. I'm going wherever Jesus goes." Not, "Watch me, because I have it all together."

As long as we are charging after Christ as quickly and closely as possible, we will always have a ton to offer to those we are leading. When we're headed for trouble is when we limit them to our own knowledge and understanding by trying to lead in our own efforts.

#P31Prayer

God, help me do things in Your order. I know that I am so easily distracted. Help me to focus on what matters most. I want my actions to show that I am actively pursuing my family and those you have entrusted to me. Protect me against thinking that I must have it all together in myself. It's You who holds all things together, not any of my own ideas or expectations. Don't let me live a life that tries to do everything independently of You and others. Consume my heart. Surround me with others who are better than I am and who push me closer to You. For those who fall under my leadership, give me a heart that follows You first and serves them second. I know that if I will focus my leadership efforts on those two things, I will be following the example of Jesus. I wouldn't have any talents or abilities if it weren't for You, so I submit them back to You for Your use. Anything You have put inside me, use it for Your glory and Your fame. Help me to follow You closely and quickly. We love you. Amen.

#P31Practice

I'll confess: I'm tired of people saying that leadership is lonely. Yes, it's trying. Yes, it's difficult. Of course, we will likely be misunderstood by many. And while I would never try to say that there won't be moments where you will feel lonely, it's completely backwards of our Savior's example to believe that leadership requires a lonely life.

No one will ever be more misunderstood than Jesus. Try to place yourself back in that time. What would it be like to wrap your mind around a man, born of a virgin, teaching with authority as the Son of God, who chose disciples that were ordinary men, not the religious elite?

But as the only one truly in a category where no one on Earth was capable of understanding His exact position, Jesus still did not go through life alone. He did not shut others out. He was fully God, but He still prioritized companionship and doing life alongside others.

If Jesus, the One God, proclaimed as the Name above all other names, let people into His life, we are without excuse. If we choose to be lonely leaders, it's exactly that: a choice, not a sacrificial requirement of leadership.

Refuse to live your life alone. Go through the necessary effort to dig into life with others. Change the culture. You'll be amazed how much further your leadership will multiply when you couple leadership with a genuine heart that cares, overflowing with acts of service.

My favorite definition of ministry is from Dave Earley: "Ministry is getting dirty to make others clean."

Getting dirty from serving those we lead is evidence that we're leaving an eternity-driven legacy behind.

How can I better serve and do life alongside those God has placed in my life?

____

____

____

____

____

____

day ten

#P31Goal

I make prayerful, calculated decisions that reflects God's timing.

#P31Authority

*She **considers a field** and buys it; From her earnings, she plants a vineyard.* Proverbs 31:16

#P31Encouragement

I love that God's Word has no wasted words. I've read the Bible through in a semester while getting my master's degree. I've done several years of following a Bible reading plan in order to get through the entire Bible in a year.

But I'm also a huge fan of slow, intentional study, making sure we fully take the time to digest every word.

For example, if we gloss over this passage too quickly, we might miss the weight found by simply using the word "considers."

"Considers" implies that she is not impulsive. She's a visionary who slows down to make sure her decisions reflect high standards and wise judgments. But because she takes careful consideration in her decisions, she's not afraid to take a calculated risk.

I'll confess: I was always a dreamer growing up. I'm grateful I had parents who recognized and encouraged this trait in me. They didn't try to squelch my childlike innocence with a "dose of reality."

Because I was always allowed to dream, I think it's made having vision as an adult much easier for me. As I work with many women to develop their businesses and ministries, I find that there aren't many who can relate to my childhood experience.

Their vision has been clouded by doubt. Plagued by "reality." Phrases spoken to them by others echo in their minds about why "that won't work" or they shouldn't "waste their time on such things."

Now, remember..."she considers." It's not leaping before you look. But we must realize that following God's will regularly requires risk.

Imagine Noah building the ark when the world had never seen rain *(Genesis 6-8)*. Or Elijah soaking the altar with water before praying for God to consume it with flames without using any fire of his own *(1 Kings 18:16-39)*. Or Barnabus walking into the apostles' house with Saul, whom we may know as a warrior for Christ and author of the majority of the New Testament, but they just knew as a persecutor of Christians *(Acts 9:26-27)*.

We must balance our fear of risk with the reality that we are always safer in God's will than we are out of it. Remember Jonah? He ran from God's call to go to Nineveh, and he ended up spending three days in the belly of a whale.

So here's my personal "Consider" process:

• ***Pause***

Unless I have a "burning bush moment" with God, my husband

has asked me on a date, or my kids want to snuggle, very few things get my immediate "yes." Even if it's a great opportunity, I've learned that I can't trust my own excitement, and I need to make sure that that opportunity or choice aligns with my priorities, my current responsibilities and my season of life.

• *Pray*

I've made decisions in my life without God, and it's never gotten me anywhere I wanted to be. We are all in desperate need of His infinite wisdom. His Word promises us that when we lack wisdom, we just need to ask, and He will give it generously *(James 1:5)*.

Have you ever attempted to use an appliance in your house and found that it wasn't working? You troubleshoot, you Google, you search for the box and get annoyed that you have to make a trip to the store to make a return...and in your attempt to place the broken piece of junk back in said box, you realize that it simply wasn't plugged into the wall!

(Totally hypothetical story, of course. Never happened to me. Especially never happened twice! ☺*)*

But that's what we do when we expect something to work without praying. We don't have a right to be frustrated if we're simply not plugged into our Power Source.

Even if a direct answer doesn't come immediately, prayer is always a relief because prayer is a transfer of power. It's a humble heart that admits, "God, I can't, but You can."

• *Pace*

After we've paused and prayed, God can direct our pace. Even if we've got a vision from God, we still have to pray for His timing. We want to carefully be in tune with Him. We want to be in step with the Spirit, not sprinting ahead or lagging behind.

I often ask the question, "God, is this is a 'glimpse' or a 'go'?" Meaning, "Is this something you're showing me for later, or is this something You're calling me to do now?"

Then, after she considers, she "buys." She takes action.

Faith is not a sideline sport. None of us is called to be a spectator. We all have different positions, but we're all in the game.

God doesn't call any of us to be benchwarmers.

We must realize that if God has called us to do something, and we remain inactive, that's not just passive. It's not just playing it safe.

Inaction when God has called you to action is disobedience. We must stop thinking that disobedience only comes when we do a wrongful behavior.

Think about it. Has your child ever gotten into trouble because you asked them to come to You and they refused to move? Or maybe you spoke to them and they refused to answer?

We can see it clearly when we are the authority, but we are often guilty of ignoring God's promptings on our hearts.

It doesn't have to be huge. Maybe he's not calling you to consider and buy property. But maybe there's a ministry in your church where you know you should be serving. Or there's a new mom in town, and you know she needs a friend. Maybe you just encounter a random stranger, and all you need to do is offer them your smile.

Pause. Pray. Pace.

#P31Prayer

God, we thank You for your wisdom, and we thank You that you never withhold it from us. Forgive us when we try and struggle on our own without plugging into You. Help us to avoid impulsivity. Give us good instincts, but help us to put on the brakes if our tendency is to jump too quickly. Help us to turn to You in prayer, not as a last resort, but as our first response. Give us the humility to realize that any knowledge that we have is from You, and that you have infinitely more wisdom than we will ever be capable to obtain. Make us disciplined to seek You in regular prayer, and not just when we need something. We should not only confess our struggles in our presence, but you should be our first place to celebrate any success, since You are the Giver of all good gifts. Give us confidence to take calculated risks at the appropriate time. Ensure that it's not false confidence in ourselves, but true confidence in You. Confirm in our hearts that You will always do what You say you will do. Finally, pace us to know when to stop, when to have patience, and when to pursue. We know You are the Rock who won't move, so God, we pray in advance for the wisdom to continually draw near to You. Thank you for being our Constant. We love you. Amen.

#P31Practice

Think about a vision God has given you for your life. Pray God will remove any preconceptions and doubts in your mind. Then, journal through the "Pause, Pray, Pace" steps on paper. You may not be able to get through all three steps today, but continuously come back and add pages to your prayer journal until you're certain that you have a clear answer from God. Once you have His answer, spring into action, wait, or stop. I am already celebrating Your obedience to Him!

God's vision for my life:

___

___

___

___

Pause:

Pray:

Pace:

day eleven

#P31Goal

I must make the most of the resources, investments, and opportunities God has entrusted to me.

#P31Authority

She considers a field ***and buys it; From her earnings, she plants*** *a vineyard.* Proverbs 31:16

#P31Encouragement

Just the mention of money stirs up many emotions. But let's remember: this isn't talking about the right to shop or about making more money. Our concern is observing her character through how she handles money.

The first thing we see is that she acts responsibly with her family's money. More than how much she earns or contributes to her family's finances, the big picture is simply that she is trustworthy.

As we discovered yesterday, this was a prayerful, wise decision, not an impulsive purchase. In fact, we can already see that she has thought about what she will do with her investment: she plants a vineyard.

When she purchased the land, she already had a plan for what she would do with it. Because she chose a vineyard, we can see she is making investments that will not just benefit her now, but will benefit her family in the future.

Trustworthy doesn't stop at simply not draining our family's finances for something we want now. Trustworthy means that the way we spend money reflects a heart that actively works to benefit our family's future.

She has a long-term plan for her earnings that greatly surpasses her own needs and wants. Again, this has less to do with how much money we make, but simply with how we handle the money we have.

When it comes to living the Christian life, money might be one of the most misunderstood issues. There are two truths we must navigate between when it comes to money.

- ***Truth #1: It is the love of money that is evil, not money itself. (1 Timothy 6:10)***

Money, in itself, is amoral. There are some people who handle having large amounts of money well and do many good things with their money. Typically, these are the people who realize that everything belongs to God. As Randy Alcorn put it so eloquently, we are merely stewards of the resources God has entrusted to us, not owners.[4]

Money is a resource from God. Money can be used to do many good things. Money can send people on mission trips to advance the gospel. Money can buy Bibles so that people have access to read God's Word. Money can provide food for the hungry, shelter for

---

[4] Alcorn, Randy. *The Treasure Principle: Unlocking the Secret of Joyful Giving*

the homeless, and clothing for the poor. Money enables pulpits to be filled every Sunday with pastors who have had time to spend studying God's Word to give God's message to us. Money builds churches, orphanages, hospitals, etc.

Yet, the very same dollar bill that can go toward good can also contribute to evil. It can be used to load up on "stuff" to impress others or gain worldly status. It can be withheld from tithing, insisting that we "worked hard" or "earned it for ourselves." Money can even contribute to addiction, abuse, prostitution and pornography.

The fact still remains that the problem isn't with money. Whether goodness shines or trouble stirs depends upon who is handling the money.

• ***Truth #2: Money may not be evil, but it is still dangerous.*** The reality remains: more people love money than don't love money. So how might we know if we are headed toward the love of money with our lives?

The answer is just a few verses ahead in 1 Timothy 6:6-7: "But godliness ***with contentment*** is great gain. For we brought nothing into the world, and we can take nothing out of it."

Have you ever met anyone who is content with how much money they make? If you ask someone who makes $40,000/year what constitutes a rich man, he will tell you that it's a man who makes $80,000. Six-figure earners will say millionaires. Millionaires will say billionaires.

The love of money shows its first sprouts when we feel those seeds of discontentment in our hearts. And while the word "discontentment" may not sound too evil, think of it this way.

Discontentment is really our heart saying, "God, everything You've given me and everything You've done for me is not enough."

Contentment is the key to keeping our money-mindset in check.

Need something more concrete? Jesus put it this way: *"It is easier for a camel to go through the eye of a needle than for a rich person to enter the Kingdom of God"* (Matthew 19:24).

Quite the visual picture, huh? Turns out, Biggie Smalls was a theologian when he said, "Mo' Money, Mo' Problems!" (Kidding... kind of.)

I may be young, but in my short life and business career, I've already seen great people turn for the worse when they began making money. They turn from dependence on God to falsely believing they can depend on themselves. They see more money as an opportunity to do more for themselves more than as an opportunity to do more for others.

Charles Swindoll once said, "If God has opened the floodgates of blessing and you are making money, don't flaunt it. Ask Him what it's for."

So to help myself balance the two extremes, this is the definition of money I've started using for myself:

> ***Money is one of the resources God gives us, and each day we must make the decision whether we will use that resource for His glory or our own.***

#P31Prayer

God, forgive me for the times I've shown my love for money and stuff more clearly than I've shown my love for You. I know there has been evidence in my life of discontentment. I pray You would step in and fill me. You have placed a void in my life that can only be filled by You. If I ever start to love money more than You, I pray that You would decrease my income. No money, achievement, status or stuff is worth distancing myself from You. But God, should I be faithful with my little and You decide to give me more, keep me grounded in You just the same. Rather than increasing my spending or my lifestyle, help me to increase my generosity. Help me to view money as a resource that You've given me, and give me the wisdom to choose to use that resource much more for Your glory than my own. We love you. Amen!

#P31Practice

Do you view money as defined by today's lesson? Sit down with your finances, and evaluate the following questions. (For best results, sit down with your spouse, and complete this exercise together!)

Do I view money in my bank account as mine or as God's?

____

____

____

____

What does the way I spend my money say about how I value God?

____

____

____

____

Am I trustworthy with my family's finances?

Do I make financial purchases with others in mind more than myself?

Are there any seeds of discontentment in my life I need to cut off?

day twelve

#P31Goal

I recognize that to best take care of them, I must also take care of me.

#P31Authority

She girds herself with strength and makes her arms strong. Proverbs 31:17

#P31Encouragement

If you know my story, you know that I can't let this verse go by without giving a shout-out to the importance of health and fitness. In fact, I love this verse so much that when I first launched my faith and fitness clothing line, Cross Training Couture, this was the very first verse I ever put on a tank top. *(But I promise, I'll contain my personal story as much as possible and keep this about her character!)*

We can't ignore that this passage does refer to her physical body because her arms are mentioned. But notice, this doesn't say, "She works hard and makes herself skinny/sexy/hot/whatever futile word you wish to insert here." She's not in it to be thin or achieve some worldly standard of physical attractiveness.

In case you don't know my story, I did this very wrong in the past. In fact, I put my own life in danger to be thin. I was not driven by the right motivations. I didn't care about being strong. I just wanted to be skinny. I just wanted to be considered beautiful. And I wanted it all for my own glory.[5]

Thankfully, God got ahold of my life, restored me, and gave me a second chance. I still work out regularly, but it's no longer obsessive. My focus is no longer about looking a certain way, but making sure that I can keep up with my life's demands.

Consider this: Wouldn't it be tragic if God called us to do something, but we were not in the physical condition to accomplish it?

I now view my workouts as a spiritual act of worship. They're a way of showing my commitment to His call on my life. It's a response of obedience. I realize there are elements of health that are beyond our control, but we can be intentional to ensure that we don't have physical limitations that are our own doing.

So forget that pant size and swimsuit season. Let's equip ourselves to be strong as best as we can. Let's increase our chances of being ready to obey God fully and to go after anything He has in store for us.

"Strength" and "strong" are the words of choice here...and this where her character shines through.

We're not even halfway through our study together, and we already know one thing for sure: Girlfriend has stuff to do! And strength is required. No wimps allowed. She is a strong woman, and she's not afraid of the hard work she needs to do to accomplish her goals.

---

[5] Myers, Michelle. *The Look that Kills: An Anorexic's Addition to Control*

After all, strength is an indicator of what we can do, not what we look like in the mirror. Physical strength doesn't happen overnight. And it can't be developed and increased without action. Consistent action.

The athletes with the best performance are also the most disciplined in their training. Discipline and performance go hand-in-hand.

Are discipline and consistency easy? No. Everyone wants to shine in performance; much fewer are actually willing to put in the behind-the scenes work required.

I never want to paint the picture that this is simple. We often quote Hebrews 12:11 in reference to discipline for disobedience, but if we look on to verses 12-13, we can see both meanings of discipline covered here:

> *So take a new grip with your tired hands and strengthen your weak knees. Mark out a straight path for your feet so that those who are weak and lame will not fall but become strong.* Hebrews 12:12-13 (NLT)

Reading this, I'm reminded of an encouraging coach, who reminds us that the stronger we get personally, the more we can benefit the team.

So, Mamas, let's break this down simply for us. Taking time to care for ourselves does not make us selfish. Now, can this be abused? As with anything, certainly.

We must ensure that our motives remain pure. If our commitment to our health is rooted in the desire to be strong, to be ready for God's call and to strengthen others, we can protect ourselves from self-obsession.

How can we know if our health routine is healthy for us and those around us? Here's my simple rule:

> ***Our health routine should enhance, not hinder, our lives.***

If our workouts have us at the gym for hours a day and other areas of our lives are suffering, it's no longer enhancing our lives. If our workouts are so strenuous that we are often too tired or too sore to play a game of tag with our kids, it's no longer enhancing our lives. If Mommy consistently doesn't eat with the family, or our meal schedule sucks the joy out of everyday living, it's no longer enhancing our lives.

On the other side of the equation, if we've allowed ourselves to get so heavy that we can't get down on the floor to do a puzzle with our child, we are not enhancing our lives. If we're consistently at the doctor because our immune systems don't have the proper nutrients to function, we are not enhancing our lives. If our lifestyle choices have created so many health complications that we've increased our risk factors for numerous fatal diseases, we're not enhancing our lives.

Those are hard, but simple facts, and they lead to easy evaluation of our own routines. Taking care of yourself, when done with the correct motives, should best equip you to take care of others.

#P31Prayer

God, we confess that it's often so hard to remain pure in this area. Everywhere we turn, false expectations of health exist. This world has complicated it and twisted it so much that it's easy to overlook our health in the temptation to give in to the world's cheap version of beauty. With that mindset, we also overlook the opportunity to show our devotion to You with our discipline. Renew our minds and open our eyes to Your truth. Give us the discipline required to pursue strength. Keep our motives pure to ensure that our health habits point us closer to You and enhance the gift of the lives that You've given us. Help us to utilize our strength to further Your name and to strengthen others. Help us to see lasting results – not results we'll find in the mirror or on the scale – but results of more energy and strength to take care of those You have graciously entrusted to us. We love you. Thank You for being in the smallest details. Amen.

#P31Practice

Does your health routine enhance or hinder your life? Does it better equip you to tackle God's call and to strengthen others? Ask the tough questions, and make the necessary steps toward improvement. It won't happen overnight, but small steps of improvement are still steps of obedience. There's no step of obedience that's too small to go unnoticed by our God.

No matter which side of the equation you land on, I've found this prayer to be extremely helpful to pray before each workout that I do. Some have told me it's silly to pray before my workout. I say it's silly to consistently do anything that we don't invite God to participate in.

Here's my prayer:

> ***"God, use this workout to make me physically capable of whatever task You need me to accomplish. More than calorie-burning, fat-blasting, or cellulite-shedding, let it be an action that shows my heart's willingness and openness to serve You whenever and wherever You need me."***[6]

[6] Myers, Michelle. *Cross Training Devos, Volume 1*

Does my health routine enhance or hinder my life?

Does my health routine better equip me to tackle God's call and strengthen others?

My Health Prayer:

____

____

____

____

____

____

____

day thirteen

#P31Goal

I prioritize personal integrity when making wise business decisions.

#P31Authority

She senses that her gain is good; Her lamp does not go out at night.
Proverbs 31:18

#P31Encouragement

When I mentor Christian women in business, one of the common troubles that comes up is guilt when it comes to asking for someone's business. Truly, it boils down to feeling guilty for asking someone for their money.

Wayne Grudem describes an honest business transaction as

one "when both parties are better off after the transaction is over."[7]

For simplicity's sake, let's use an example. A family decides that they only need one car, so they decide to sell their second car. The car is in good condition. But with their recent decision of transitioning from being a dual-income-family to a single-income-family, since the wife just had their first baby, having the extra income would benefit them more than a second vehicle. They sell their car to a family of a fifteen-year-old who will be getting his license next week.

The seller's family is better off because they have the extra needed income. The buyer's family is better off because they have another car, since their family now has one extra driver. All parties are better off from this business transaction.

One small change could make this a bad business deal. What if the car had major engine troubles that the seller didn't disclose to the buyer? Then, the buyer is not better off, because they're not getting the quality vehicle they were promised, and they will be out additional money to repair the faulty car.

I'll give some specifics to my business women in a minute, but let's go big picture. What does this Proverbs 31:18 teach us about this woman's character?

She prioritizes personal integrity.

A verse that comes to my mind is 1 Corinthians 10:31: *"Whether you eat or drink, or whatever you do, do it all to the glory of God."*

Having integrity means that, from the big moments of life, to the small, seemingly insignificant ones (like what we choose to eat and drink) we should have God's glory on our minds. Integrity doesn't just come into play when dealing with money or closing a business deal.

> *We can have integrity by refusing to participate in gossip.*
>
> *We can have integrity by apologizing to our children*

---

[7] Grudem, Wayne. *Business for the Glory of God: The Bible's Teachings on the Moral Goodness of Business*

when we lose our tempers.

We can have integrity by admitting to our husbands when we are wrong. (I know my husband will underline that last one when he reads this!)

We can have integrity by not exaggerating our achievements.

We can have integrity by being real about our struggles, rather than faking our way through life.

We can have integrity by citing our sources within our social media content, instead of trying to pass off another person's words as our own.

Integrity matters.

For my business ladies, let me give a few tips I learned from Michael Hyatt, creator of Platform University, that have helped me in realizing that charging for our products and services and participating in mutually-beneficial business transactions is actually improving the experience of those we are serving.[8]

- ***You will produce better services/products.***

If there's no fee, there's no accountability tying you to producing a higher-quality product. Knowing people are paying you for a product and service will increase your attention to make sure the quality of what they are receiving is worth paying for.

- ***You will be able to go deeper.***

When I first launched She Works His Way, we were simply a social media platform. I only ran it through Facebook and Instagram for our first 18 months. I didn't even have a website. I was completely at the mercy of Mark Zuckerberg. If either of those platforms shut down, I would have completely lost the community we were

---

[8] http://michaelhyatt.com/paid-content-benefits.html

working to build.

In addition, as numbers began to grow and demands of what our community wanted increased, I began spending money that I was earning through another business to provide She Works His Way with the tools and resources we needed, like a webinar service and an administrative assistant.

Again, if the other business had gone under, She Works His Way would have been vulnerable.

I was very anxious about becoming a membership community. But once we did it, I was able to breathe a deep sigh of relief. Not only did I have a more reliable mode of reaching our target audience, but we were giving the ministry room to grow and to expand for the future.

- ***You have more resources to grow.***

Not only did launching a membership community for She Works His Way give me a more reliable mode of reaching our target audience, but with financial support, we now had room for the ministry to grow and expand.

In August 2016, our She Works His Way, "swHw," app will launch. That's something that would not have been financially possible without the funding supplied by our members and our mentorship students.

Yes, we could have asked for donations. But we didn't, so I don't know how that the story would have ended. However, I also know that God has blessed She Works His Way with an incredible staff that have beautiful hearts and serious skill. Instead of just asking for a donation, I love that we've been able to give our community something valuable in return for their money.

Rest easy, sweet sister. With integrity, we can know that any gain we experience is for good overall, both for us and for others.

#P31Prayer

God, help my character to keep personal integrity on display at all times. In big things and small moments that no one sees, help me to make decisions that bring You glory. If You can't get glory from it, God, then I don't want to be anywhere near it. Give me the wisdom to pursue all business endeavors with a spirit of excellence. Help me to take the definition of a good business transaction one step further, and rather than just making sure both parties are better off, to run my business in such a way that it both underpromises and overdelivers. I want my buyer to benefit even more than I do, Lord. Give me peace in the calling that You have given me. Position the ministries and endeavors that You have entrusted me with to grow Your name. Guide my heart, and keep my motives pure. Reassure me consistently that my gain is good. We love you. Amen.

#P31Practice

Have you ever "met" someone on social media who you just immediately thought, "If she lived next door, we would be inseparable." You're totally inspired by everything she does. She's coming to speak in your town, you get super excited, you arrange a meeting with her....and then in person, you discover she's nothing like her online personality?

A huge piece of integrity is authenticity. Social media has created somewhat of a "virtual life" for some people. It's a place where their husbands always say the right thing and bring roses home for no reason, kids ace the big test and hit a homerun in the same day. Life is just breezy. The day that her kid colored on the walls with Sharpie somehow missed the highlight reel...and so did that argument with her spouse.

Now, I'm not saying that we should vomit our lives on social media. I'm a big believer in changing the question Facebook asks from, "What's on your mind?" to "What can I share that will inspire others to want me as an influential part of their lives?" And if the Facebook algorithm is so smart, I'm waiting for the day when status updates can be rejected if they don't answer that question!

But, too many times, I see women who are so consumed with

creating an online appearance that they're neglecting the real life that's happening right in front of them.

So here's my challenge for those of you in leadership attempting to use social media as an outlet for influence:

Live better offline to be better online.

We are not virtual beings, so attempting to live a virtual life is not just silly – it's impossible.

If we are consumed with living service-focused lives with the people God has placed in our actual path, then we will be able to extend that inspiration to those who are connected to us virtually.

However, if we make it our goal for our online life to appear better than our real life, we will be sucked down into vortex of constant disappointment. No matter how great it is, the virtual cannot overshadow the mediocre (or worse) reality in front of us.

So today, let's recommit to live better offline. Love deeper. Care more. Serve with greater enthusiasm. Lead with more authenticity. Do more with intention and excellence. Basically, let's pursue a greater purpose than our selfish gain.

Only then can we take a deep sigh of relief and praise the One who gave us our assignments and our platform in the first place.

How will I live better offline?

day fourteen

#P31Goal

My purpose always trumps my preference.

#P31Authority

She senses that her gain is good; ***Her lamp does not go out at night.***
Proverbs 31:18

#P31Encouragement

Aren't you glad that we started our character study together by breaking down that P31 isn't a job description? Between rising when it is still dark and having a lamp that doesn't go out at night, I'm thinking exhaustion and an emotional breakdown would be right around the corner if we took this literally!

Here's our character takeaway: She consistently extends her energy for good, and she is never off-duty for the people and the priorities that are most important to her.

Her purpose trumps her preference.

I've already confessed to you that I'm rarely jazzed for my 5am wake-up call. But spending time with my Savior and carving out some time for self-care trump my preference of sleeping in.

I don't love being awakened in the middle of the night by a crying child. But nursing my newborn or providing comfort to my toddler who had a nightmare have a deeper place in my heart than my desire for an uninterrupted night of sleep.

It's not easy. Even though I know the purpose is much greater than any personal preference, it's still a challenge.

Bigger than that, it's a great opportunity to adopt the mindset of Jesus, as we *"in humility, value others above ourselves, not looking to your own interests but each of you to the interests of others"* (Philippians 2:3-4).

It's these selfless moments that provide us with a wonderful opportunity to reflect Jesus to our families and to others around us.

Humility is one of those traits that is often misunderstood. C.S. Lewis said it best: "True humility is not thinking less of yourself; it is thinking of yourself less."

Have you ever known a "martyr mother"? This is a woman who consistently dwells on the sacrifices that she makes for her family. Sometimes, it comes across as "super holy." Other times, it presents itself as passive aggression.

But that is not humility. Real humility is a lot like your underwear – it shouldn't show! Think about it: Jesus didn't brag about what He was going to do at the cross or throw His sacrifice in the disciples' faces after His resurrection.

Just like our Savior, we should serve others out of the overflow of our love for God. Not out of guilt, obligation, or drudgery. Not for sympathy or applause.

Think about how opposite this is from what we're largely taught in the world. We're taught to do the things that make us happy and/or impress others. (Bonus if you can do them both at the same time!)

One other example from Jesus that helps us live this out: Philippians 2:7 describes how He laid down His deity and humbled Himself to take on human form. On earth, He was still very much God, but He laid down His rights so that He could be human for us.

He laid down His rights. We don't have to wonder what His preference was. As He prayed in the Garden before His betrayal and crucifixion, "He fell with His face to the ground and prayed, 'My Father, if it is possible, may this cup be taken from Me. Yet not as I will, but as You will.'"

No doubt, He would have preferred to defeat sin with His deity alone, rather than an excruciating death. But He laid down His preference for a greater purpose. He laid down His preference for you and me. He laid down His preference to walk in obedience to God.

If Jesus can lay down His deity to face an underserved death, I'm pretty sure it makes any of our examples seem pretty petty in comparison.

What "rights" have you hung onto that you may need to let go of in order to embrace your current season and His call on your life?

Let's see the big picture: Every time we lay down our preference for God's purposes, we are reflecting the attitude of Jesus. We are allowing fruit to form in our lives, which gives others glimpses of God as we go against the natural human impulse of selfishness.

Purpose > Preference. May we be those kind of women!

#P31Prayer

God, help us to lay down our will for Yours. Help us to prioritize Your plans and Your purposes for us over our comfort and our preferences. May we seek Your heart in all circumstances. Help us to be present and active where You have called us to be. If we're honest, we admit that it's so much easier to be served than to serve. But don't let us fall victim to the lie that serving is not more enjoyable. God, we know Your Word is true when You tell us it is more blessed to give than to receive *(Acts 20:35)*. Push us into our uncomfortable zone as we seek out opportunities to serve others with an attitude that reflects Your Son's. Help us to follow in His example, choosing Your purposes and laying down any "rights" that we may selfishly feel we deserve. Help us to remember that selfishness ruins love, and that humility builds love. We lay down our rights. We lay down our preferences. Consider this prayer as an offering of obedience: We are never off-duty for You, the family You have entrusted to us, and Your call on our lives. We're all in. Your way over our way, every time. We love you so much. Amen.

#P31Practice

In Luke 9:23, Jesus instructed us, *"If any of you wants to be My follower, you must turn from your selfish ways, take up your cross daily and follow me."* Let's spend some time journaling today, breaking down His instruction. Let's beg Him to speak about what specifically He wants us to do in our lives by journaling answers to these three questions:

What selfishness in my life do I need to turn away from?

____

____

____

What cross have you called me to pick up? How will I serve you by serving others?

How do I ensure that my focus is not on me leading others, but instead is consumed with following Jesus?

---

day fifteen

#P31Goal

No matter the task, my strong work ethic remains.

#P31Authority

She ***stretches*** *out her hands to the* ***distaff****, and her hands* ***grasp*** *the* ***spindle****.* Proverbs 31:19

#P31Encouragement

Even if you sew as part of your job or your hobby, I doubt you use a distaff or a spindle anymore. Humor me while I explain these tools, even if it's just for myself. *(Because I happen to be so domestically challenged in this area that I may have used a hot glue gun to put a button back on one of my husband's shirts!)*

These were the basic tools required for spinning, where three different fibers are spun together and converted into yarn. Yarn becomes fabric. Fabric becomes textiles. Then, textiles are made into clothing.

I don't have to be a seamstress to know that this is behind-the-scenes grunt work. However, I did do a quick Google search to find a picture of a distaff and a spindle. The tool looks like a broom, with the distaff at the top and the spindle at the very bottom. Not only was this task tedious, but I'm sure holding your hands in that position was less than uncomfortable.

We have so much to learn about her character here. Let's start with the obvious: There's no task beneath her.

How many of us volunteer for the behind-the-scenes grunt work? Does anyone ever say, "I would absolutely love to stack the chairs after today's meeting!"? Or "Can I please do the dishes?" Then, there's my personal favorite: "Oooh, dibs on that dirty diaper!"

We've only begun to dig into this amazing woman, but we can already see that she's pretty successful. The typical progression we see as people grow in their influence is that more and more tasks fall on others, and they only stick to the higher profile items.

Let me be clear: I have zero problems with delegation. I love outsourcing to people who are better than I am at certain tasks. I also recognize that there are simply some responsibilities I have that someone else can do so that I have the time to do other things.

Can do, though. Not *should* do. Or *has to* do.

Again, it goes back to one thing: attitude. Our attitude in delegation matters. Here's the bottom line: If you believe a task is somehow beneath you, that belief will translate into thinking (even if you never voice it out loud) that the person who does that task for you is somehow beneath you, too.

> *Now there are a variety of gifts, but the same Spirit. And there are varieties of ministries, and the same Lord.* 1 Corinthians 12:4-5

Yes, this is about us having different gifts, but it's really showing us our unity. God was every bit as purposeful in giving me my gifts as He was in giving you yours. Of course, our gifts are different, but that doesn't mean that one of us got his primary attention while the other got His leftovers.

God doesn't play that way. The opposite is true.

The apostle Paul explained it this way: *"In His grace, God has given us different gifts for doing things well"* (Romans 12:6).

In His grace. Grace flows out of His goodness. He is good to give us different gifts) because, if we all had the same gifts, we wouldn't need one another. We wouldn't have reason to work together. We wouldn't collectively represent the Body of Christ and serve as one *(1 Corinthians 12:27).*

How do we know that the P31 woman had this kind of attitude? Because of the use of the words *stretches* and *grasps*. This is not half-hearted effort. She is giving this task all she's got.

This is Ecclesiastes 9:10 in action: *"Whatever your hand finds to do, do it with all your might. For when you go to the grave, there will be no work, planning, knowledge or wisdom."*

Doesn't that fill you with a sense of urgency? Today is a gift, and tomorrow is not promised. We have to act now. It might not be tomorrow, but we do have a time limit. We must ensure that we are acting now with the tasks that we have been given today. Because "tomorrow," whether we mean that literally or as "someday," may never arrive.

Let me be really vulnerable with you. I tried to outsource the writing of this very project. I taught through this passage, and I thought that it would be a great idea to let someone take my teaching and turn it into a book. After all, they would still be my thoughts. It would simply be someone else doing the typing.

I hired someone, and the task was completed. All I needed to do was edit, and it was done! But through a series of events, God convicted my heart that I couldn't use that version of the project. He asked me to start over and to do it myself.

This meant a lot of things. Not only did this push back my release date and ministry plan (that we prayed over and had already put into motion), but it meant that I had to recreate that plan from scratch, continue what was already in motion, and somehow squeeze this assignment in, too.

I'll admit it; I was less than thrilled at the beginning. After all, I had paid someone else to do this already. You name it, I griped about it. From "it wasn't efficient" to "it wasn't fair," I used them all.

Thankfully, before I began, God gave me the presence of mind to pray for an attitude adjustment. I prayed Colossians 3:23 until my attitude calibrated in line with His assignment: *"Whatever you do, work at it with all your heart, as working for the Lord, and not for human masters."*

Oh, sweet sister. Can I just tell you the blessing I would have missed out on if I had missed writing this project? God has shown me so much. He has convicted me. I've learned new things. I've gotten fresh words and challenges from Him. Though many of the circumstances that led to my writing this were some of the hardest attacks I have gone through in ministry, they were all worth it, if for nothing else than gaining some of the sweetest moments I've ever had at our Savior's feet.

But it doesn't stop there. This one step of obedience was a catalyst for a myriad of blessings that I could never have orchestrated on my own. I would love to have heard God's laughter amidst my complaints and whining.

In fact, I think I will make a note at the front of my prayer journal that says, "Simmer down, child. Just give me a bit. Stay close to Me because I'm about to blow your mind." Then, I can just refer to it as necessary.

Maybe you're in a season where you have some pretty undesirable job circumstances. Maybe you're extremely frustrated in your current season of life. I can't change your circumstances, and maybe you can't either.

But choosing to have a joyful attitude and choosing Whom we will serve is always our choice to make. When we change our perspective from, "I have to do this because of [something for me] to "He has called me here to do this for Him," we have tapped into the only unlimited power that exists.

We may not be able to do anything in our own strength, but He can do anything in His! If we are willing to let Him work through us, even if we have no idea how or what He will do, He has the ability to blow us away with His purpose every single time.

All He needs is a willing and obedient heart.

See how our simplest actions and attitudes have the power to reflect or deflect God's glory?

Let's stretch. Let's grasp. Let's do whatever our hands find to do as if working for Him, wherever we find ourselves today.

Then, let's wait expectantly for God to show up and do what only He can do.

#P31Prayer

God, the very fact that You are listening to us right now proves that You have already gone before us, displaying this trait in Your character. Your Word describes that You bend down to listen to us *(Psalm 116:2)*. Give us that posture, Lord. Help us bend down to serve You and serve others, whenever and however You desire to use us. Help us to realize that we are ultimately serving You with our actions. We may not always love or understand our circumstances, God, but help us never to doubt Your purpose in it and through it all. Put Your joy on display in us. Help us to recognize the gifts and abilities that You have given others. May we never view our gifts as superior or inferior to the gifts that You have given to other people. All gifts come from You, and You do not play favorites. Thank you for displaying Your grace to us and to a lost world by making us function better together. Unify us, Lord, so we are an accurate picture of You to those who do not yet know You. We trust You in all things, and we love You. Amen.

#P31Practice

Today, let's evaluate our actions and attitudes in our current season. Based on what we've learned from the character of the

P31 woman today, what do we need to work on? Do we need to work on our own work ethic? Our attitude in delegation? Let's spend some extra time in prayer, asking God to reveal how we can improve to best mimic these character traits in our lives.

Let's take this one step further and encourage someone else. Think of someone who has a completely different set of gifts than yours. Take five minutes to write them a quick note of how you see God reflected in the way they serve.

BONUS Challenge: Complete a task that normally belongs to someone else. Maybe it's handling someone else's responsibility at work. Maybe we do one of our children's chores, or a household task that normally falls under our husband. Not to get noticed. Not because we desire their appreciation. But let's do this simply to stretch and grasp to serve on behalf of someone else. Let's go beyond our call of duty and what is required in order to serve someone else well. Expect the unexpected: You will experience a greater blessing than you anticipated.

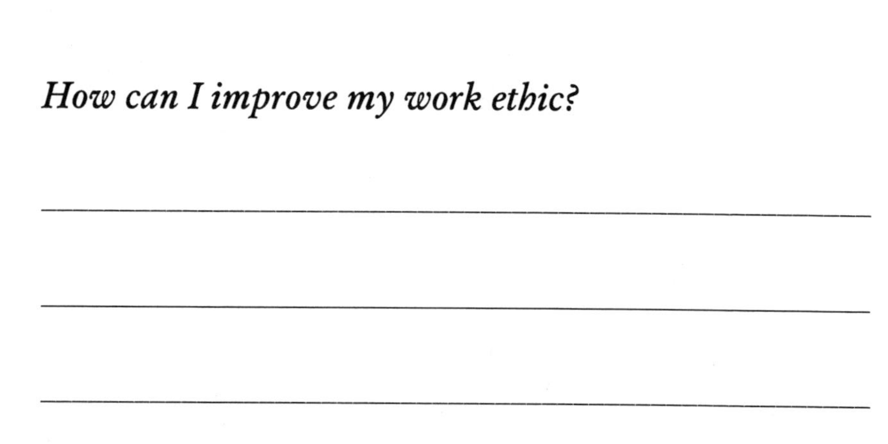

How can I improve my work ethic?

What's my attitude in delegation? Anything I need to adjust?

My Prayer Commitment:

day sixteen

#P31Goal

I give generously with pure motives.

#P31Authority

She extends her hand to the poor, *and she* ***stretches out her hands to the needy.*** Proverbs 31:20

#P31Encouragement

Is anyone else challenged by the words *"extends"* and *"stretches"* as much as I am?

Extending implies that she's using her full reach toward a particular purpose. Let's stop and consider:

Do we give with the full reach of our ***resources*** in mind...*or do we have a limit because considering everything as available for others might require sacrifices we aren't willing to make?*

Do we give with the full reach of our ***talent*** in mind...*or is there a limit to the excellence we provide based on what's in it for us?*

Do we give with the full reach of our ***attention*** in mind...*or are we often distracted by our own selfish wants?*

Do we give with the full reach of our ***purpose*** in mind...*or do we allow ourselves to focus on succeeding in things that don't ultimately matter?*

Do we give with the full reach of our ***time*** in mind...*or do we use lack of time as an excuse when in reality we're just unwilling to make the time?*

Stretching means she is giving beyond what is comfortable. True generosity isn't just about the act of giving.

Our actions aren't really generous if we aren't stretched in the process.

Studies show that the more money people make, the less they typically give.[9] How backwards is that? While these studies refer to money, it's probably safe to assume that the same spirit toward generosity applies across their lives.

I remember a particular time when my husband and I were young in ministry. We were newly married, pursuing our masters degrees full-time. He was working full-time, and I had three part-time jobs. Our money was tight, but God always provided.

---

[9] Stanley, Andy. *How to Be Rich*

One Sunday, God put a particular family in our path. They didn't have money for groceries. And, as there are no coincidences, only divine appointments with our God, James and I had planned to go grocery shopping after church.

My faith was tested as I heard James say to the woman, "Follow us to the store. We'll take care of it this week."

By looking at our bank account, my husband's words did not make sense. The money was there this week, but I wasn't sure what that would mean for us when we got to the end of the month.

My husband reassured me, "God hasn't let us go without yet."

Confirming God's promise to care for us *(Matthew 6:26)* helped me rid my mind of "reality," and embrace real faith. As I watched this couple fill their cart, my heart was overflowing with joy.

This verse came alive to me in that moment. Handing them $20 in that moment would have been easy, but I would have walked away and forgotten about it. It's been nearly 10 years, and I still remember her face of gratitude and the tear-stains on my shirt after she hugged me.

When we give to the point of being stretched, those are the moments when we truly get to watch God at work.

Also an important detail, this woman didn't ask my husband to pay for their groceries. She asked my husband for prayer that God would provide. We see the same character reflected in Proverbs 31. By extending and reaching out to the poor and needy, the P31 woman takes the initiative to be generous. The resources to meet these needs are not easily available within her immediate reach, so she is going to them.

This character trait is also consistent with my experience. The people that often need our help the most don't ask for it. If they don't ask, that means it is our responsibility to seek out opportunities to be used by God through our generosity. When our hearts and hands are completely open, we are able to be intuitive to the needs around us, and God is able to use us to help provide for someone else.

Oh, and let's make sure we don't miss that "hands" reference in the second part of that verse. The use of the plural language shows us just how much generosity this woman has. She is not just giving a little; this reinforces the truth that she's giving with all she's got.

We can't leave this without addressing who she is serving. These verses refer to the poor and needy. Once again, let's brace ourselves for the character challenge this means for us by asking one question:

How do we treat those who can do nothing for us?

Do we treat them with respect and dignity? Do we recognize them as people? Do we look down upon them? Do we ignore them? Have we wrongly elevated ourselves as "too good" to associate with them?

If so, our character is lacking an accurate depiction of our God to the world around us. We serve a seriously generous God, so we must be serious about being generous if others are to see Him reflected in us.

Now, this passage doesn't tell us to let others take advantage of our kindness. The wording also helps us to decipher that this passage is referring to needs, not wants. We must continuously pray for God's discernment and wisdom in our generosity.

For women in business, do not misinterpret this verse to believe that you cannot charge anyone for your goods or services. Proverbs 31 is clear that she runs a business that yields a profit. She couldn't run a successful business by giving everything away and saying "yes" to everyone, no matter how outlandish their requests.

Here's the line we must walk with running businesses for God's glory:

> Can we meet the needs of everyone? *No, but we can meet some, and we should.*
>
> Can a business be successful if it's run like a charity? *No. That business plan is sure to fail. A business that operates as a charity is as certain to fail as a charity*

> *that attempts to operate as a business.*
>
> Can a business that refuses to be charitable display God's glory? *Never. Our God gives too much for giving to be absent in how we serve others.*

As we pray for generosity that extends and stretches us, let's read this charge from the apostle Paul:

> *Command those who are rich in this present world not to be arrogant nor to put their hope in wealth, which is so uncertain, but to put their hope in God, who richly provides us with everything for our enjoyment. Command them to do good, to be rich in good deeds, and to be generous and willing to share. In this way they will lay up treasure for themselves as a firm foundation for the coming age, so that they may take hold of the life that is truly life.* 1 Timothy 6:17-19

#P31Prayer

God, open our hearts to be sensitive to the needs around us. As we remember that everything is Yours, let that thought not end in our minds, but flow through our hearts and out of our actions. Release our death-grip on we have in our lives and our stuff, and help us to stretch and fully extend ourselves to be used for You. Help us to see others as You see them. Remove the worldly filters that can so easily influence our treatment of others. Don't allow us to be women who wait for needs to come to us, but let us be women who seek out opportunities to put on display the generosity You showed us first. It's easy to think that generosity is our doing, Lord, but help us not to keep any of the glory for ourselves, but to give the glory to You. You are the One who provides, Lord, not us. God, as you give us more, help us not to go with the trend of giving less, but help us to increase our generosity. Help us remember the truth that if we are not being stretched, we are not truly being generous. Thank You for your generosity to us. May our actions prove that Your generosity to us is not wasted, but increases Your Kingdom. Thank you for entrusting us with what is Yours. We love You! Amen.

#P31Practice

Perhaps you've been in a season before where giving 10% to tithe to your church was really difficult, but now, that's an easy check to write each week. Maybe instead of continuing to write an easy check, it's time to stretch yourself by increasing the percentage of what you give.

Maybe in your business, you've been so focused on the bottom line that your purpose has gotten blurry. While I wouldn't encourage you to abandon diligence in business decisions, pray for discernment on ways to display His character in your calling.

Maybe you're recently retired, or God has called you to lay down your career for this season of motherhood. What are you doing with your time? Could God get more glory from how you're spending it?

Today, I encourage you to make a game plan of how you can increase your generosity to the full "stretched" position. As your generosity increases, expect increases in personal joy, and expect God to show up in a way you weren't aware was even possible.

How can I increase my generosity to the full "stretched" position?

day seventeen

#P31Goal

In providing for my family, I am equally tough and tender.

#P31Authority

She is ***not afraid of the snow*** *for her household, For all her household are* ***clothed in scarlet.*** Proverbs 31:21

#P31Encouragement

Are you a planner? I am, perhaps to a flaw. *(Shout-out to all my people who will write something down to do that they've already done just for the satisfaction of crossing it off the list!)*

But we can't just see that the P31 woman is a planner; she's a *priority* planner. She thinks further down the road than just today, and her family has the top priority slot in her brain.

I don't know about where you live, but here in western Carolina, we would be silly not to plan for the snow. With our mountainous roads, it's smart to consider 4-wheel drive when purchasing a vehicle. By October, we'd better be stocked with winter coats, gloves and hats. We should probably own a shovel for the driveway, have a scraper for the car window, and make sure the heat is working inside our homes.

But "snow" here isn't just about that white powdery stuff that falls from the sky. The poem is drawling an analogy for any situation we can plan for in advance. Preparation is key for the P31 woman.

Think about certain "snows" that could potentially occur in your family that we can start planning for now:

Are we helping our kids hide God's Word in their hearts so that when they are on their own, they will be grounded in truth? Do we plan intentional date nights with our spouses to continue to deepen that relationship? Are we saving money slowly over time to help pay for our children's college educations or for our retirement?

There are certain "snows" in life that come without warning, but if we prepare for what we are able to anticipate, we can eliminate unnecessary fears.

It still goes deeper. The two character traits displayed in this verse are so much in contrast, that we could easily see one and miss the other. But this verse illustrates that we are boldly to embody a character that is equally as tough as it is tender.

- ***Tough***

She is not afraid. Fearless. Let's be honest. The condition of our world leaves lots of room for fear to grow in our hearts. It's pretty much impossible for me to watch the evening news or scroll the Facebook newsfeed without having feelings of fear. From health issues beyond our control, to evil people capable of doing unthinkable things to children, it's easy to embrace fear as a normal part of parenting.

In fact, when I was pregnant with my oldest, my dad made me

two promises. He said, "You will never sleep the same, and you will never pray the same." Was he ever right!

But God has not called us to fear or timidity, but to power, love and self-control *(2 Timothy 1:7).* If there were a list of verses mothers should be required to memorize, this would make my top 10!

God's power. Unconditional love. Self-control. Those three traits are undoubtedly essential for motherhood. And in order to embrace them, we must cast aside our fear and timidity.

I often meet mothers who do not view themselves as leaders. Let me set the record straight: ***If you are a mother, you are a leader.***

And to be even more transparent? Leadership is not for sissies.

So, let me put that together, just so there's no room for confusion. If you're a mother, you are a leader. And if you are a leader, you must be tough.

Because tenderness and toughness go hand-in-hand (more on that next), we can eliminate a few misconceptions quickly. Tough does not mean hard or harsh. It does not abandon grace and kindness.

Tough, in this sense, describes our willingness to do the hard things. It means we are unmovable from our top priorities and solid in what matters. Even if it requires that we do something we don't like, we know that we can tap into God's strength. Tough means that with God leading our way, we can be extraordinarily bold.

• ***Tender***

What does scarlet have to do with tenderness? Since we are looking at her character, we are looking beyond what this says about her family's color of clothing. During this time, scarlet was among the most precious of dyes that would grab on only to the best of fabrics.

This shows us that she prioritizes nurturing them in the most precious ways possible. Her intentional planning enables her to provide them with the very best.

I feel like tenderness is a character trait that we don't elevate for women today. When we hear "tender," we somehow think "weak."

"Tough" is definitely taught as a valuable trait, as is evident with the "girl boss," "boss babe" and "girl power" movements. We're taught, "Take charge, girl. Because if you don't, someone else will, and you don't want anyone to be the boss of you."

Sweet sister, please don't fall victim to that lie. We have a Boss, and His name is Jesus. Our own understanding is not a reliable source, and all of our ways are to acknowledge Him, not ourselves *(Proverbs 3:5-6).*

Submitting to Him shows our wisdom and strength. Toughness in the absence of tenderness doesn't reflect our Savior. If we limit ourselves to display only our toughness, we limit how others can see Him through us.

Let's open our eyes to what tender really means. Tenderness implies a delicate rarity. It's a display of gentle elegance.

I can't help but think about a ballerina. Their graceful movements are so captivating. They appear to float across the stage effortlessly, as though they are just weightlessly floating. But if you've ever attempted ballet, you know that is not the case. Ballet requires an insane amount of both muscular strength and control.

Tough and tender is the same. Tenderness doesn't eliminate our strength as women anymore than having grace removes the strength from ballet. Let's embrace the fullness of our toughness along with our tenderness.

What are some ways that we can simultaneously put toughness and tenderness on display? Here are 10 ideas:

- ***Tough + Tender***

Speak the truth in love *(Ephesians 4:15).*

Discipline those we love *(Hebrews 12:6).*

Consider others as more important than ourselves *(Philippians 2:3).*

Bless those who persecute and mistreat us *(Luke 6:28).*

Desire righteousness above all *(Matthew 5:6).*

Choose gratitude over boasting *(1 Corinthians 4:7).*

Let inner beauty trump outer beauty *(1 Peter 3:4).*

Consider ways to motivate others to love and good works *(Hebrews 10:24).*

Make sure our actions match our words *(Ephesians 4:1).*

Proclaim God more than we promote ourselves *(2 Corinthians 4:5).*

#P31Prayer

God, give us a joyful spirit as we plan ahead and prepare for our household. Give us wisdom to see in advance whatever "snows" we can. Help us to be diligent in our pursuit to think ahead with our family in mind. God, make us tough so that we are willing to do hard things. Help us to tap into Your strength, and give us the humility to know that we cannot do life Your way apart from You. God, in the same action in which we are tough, complement our toughness with tenderness. Protect our toughness from being harsh. In the same way that You are both the Lion and the Lamb, help us to prioritize these traits so that they work together, not apart from one another. Help us not to go the way of culture, but to take the path that leads to You. Don't let us settle for what is less than Your best for us. Above all, mold us into the best reflection of You that we can possibly be so that more will come to know You. God, with our children, help us to realize the deep impact that our witness has, even more so than our words.

May we be "because of" parents, not "in spite of" parents, so that our children boldly proclaim their love for You *because* of the example they were able to see clearly displayed in us. Move in us and through us to accomplish this in Your power. We trust You, and we love you. Amen.

#P31Practice

Since this passage is taught within the context of parenting, I can't help but think about how to be tough and tender when we discipline our kids. I feel that most parents, even parents with good intentions, have a tendency toward toughness or a tendency toward tenderness, one at the expense of the other. Either trait with the absence of the other can make for confusion for our children when it comes to discipline.

Discipline is one of those topics our world loves to debate. Because of that, I am so grateful that God is not silent about His thoughts on this topic in His Word. We must be careful that we don't allow ourselves to be more influenced by our culture than by Christ *(Colossians 2:8)*.

I had the pleasure of attending a parenting conference with Dr. Ted Tripp.[10] Here are some principles I learned from him that helped shape my attitude toward discipline and provide a great outline for an equally tough and tender philosophy. I pray they are as helpful to you as they have been to my training as a parent.

- ***Make a distinction between correction and discipline.*** If you correct your child and they comply, discipline is not necessary. Discipline is reserved for defiant behavior to correction.

- ***The goal of discipline is restoration.*** The slate is wiped clean; the situation is not held over the child's head. If the end goal is merely punishment,

---

[10] http://www.shepherdingtheheart.org

then we're not disciplining with our love for them in mind.

• ***Withholding discipline does not display love.*** If God disciplines those He loves *(Hebrews 12:3-11)*, then we are doing those we love a disservice when we neglect discipline. Life requires understanding of how to operate under authority, so home is a safe place to learn this at a young age.

How can I be more tough + tender in my life?

____

____

____

____

____

____

____

____

day eighteen

#P31Goal

Because I value the *heart* issue of modesty, the *body* issue of modesty takes care of itself.

#P31Authority

She makes ***coverings*** *for herself; her clothing is fine linen and purple.*
Proverbs 31:22

#P31Encouragement

I love that the word chosen for clothing is "coverings." She's covered. Have you ever seen a woman wearing clothes, yet she wasn't covered? The poem makes sure there's no room for confusion.

So, today, we are going to go there; we are chatting about

modesty.

But here's the thing: I'm not going to give you a set of rules. I'm not going to tell you that your dresses can't come up to a certain length or that the neckline of your shirt can't go beneath a certain point.

God set the foundation of Christianity as a relationship, not as a set of rules. Since there are few concrete instructions in this area, I believe that we have to take what He has taught us in our relationship with Him and others in order to gather the clearest view of His thoughts on this topic.

Here's the bottom line: Modesty is way more of a heart issue than a body issue. If we take care of understanding the heart issue, the body issue should take care of itself.

Let's chat about a few modesty misconceptions that I've heard given in the past. And then, I'll simply let God's Word drop the mic!

- ***It's my body. I can do what I want.***
Do you not know that your bodies are temples of the Holy Spirit, who is in you, whom you have received from God? You are not your own; you were bought at a price. Therefore, honor God with your bodies. 1 Corinthians 6:19-20

- ***If he's tempted to lust after me because of what I'm wearing, it's not fair that I have to limit myself or take the blame. That's his sin, not mine.***
Therefore, let us not pass judgment on one another any longer, but rather decide never to put a stumbling block or hindrance in the way of a brother. Romans 14:13

- ***Doesn't that infringe on my "freedom in Christ?"***
For you were called to freedom, brothers. Only do not use your freedom as an opportunity for the flesh, but through love, serve one another. Galatians 5:13

• ***Okay, I'll just say it. I like the attention. It feels good to turn heads when I walk into a room.***
For all that is in the world – the desires of the flesh and the desires of the eyes and pride in possessions – is not from the Father but is from the world. 1 John 2:16

• ***I don't want to look different from everyone else. I'd rather blend in.***
Do not be conformed to this world, but be transformed by the renewal of your mind, that by testing you may discern what is the will of God, what is good and acceptable and perfect. Romans 12:2

See? Modesty is so much more of a heart issue than a body issue.

Here are our two basic truths to ensure that our hearts embrace modesty:

• ***A heart that prioritizes modesty elevates God above herself.***
Once upon a time, I competed in pageants. That's another story for another book, but in one pageant, the opening number theme was "America." We were to wear an outfit that was patriotic.

The girl in front of me wore a form-fitting evening gown that did not leave much to the imagination. The bottom half of the dress was red and white stripes, which perfectly accentuated every curve in her body. The top half was sparkly blue, and the neckline cut down to nearly right at her bellybutton. There were two white stars very strategically placed on the top half of the dress. I'll let your imagination fill in the details.

To enter the stage, we paraded through the audience. As we were about the hit the stage, there was a man seated on the front row. When he saw this woman, I thought his eyes were going to bulge out of his face. His jaw dropped to the floor, and out loud, I heard him say, "God bless America!"

Now, you and I both know, this man's mind wasn't anywhere near thinking about God or America in that moment.

I've thought about that story many times. And while we

may never find ourselves in that exact predicament, we can ask ourselves this simple question:

> ***Does what I'm wearing distract from God getting glory?***

Before you think that I've taken this too far, let's go back to God's Word. We were created for God's glory *(Isaiah 43:7)*. So anytime we shine the spotlight on ourselves instead of God, we are literally robbing ourselves of our created purpose.

My husband put it this way: "Don't believe the lie the world is trying to sell you. A modest woman is not trying to suppress herself or her individuality. A woman who practices modesty is actually the most liberated woman, because she is the one who is confident in Whom her value comes from. This makes her confident in her calling without needing the validation of this world."

If someone is unable to think about God when they look at us, we've made a sacrifice that is too great. His glory is the point of our existence, and we must take that responsibility seriously.

We must turn more hearts toward God than we turn heads toward ourselves.

• ***A heart that prioritizes modesty elevates others before themselves.*** Are we responsible for another's sin? No. But should we be unconcerned if our actions contribute to another's sin, or can we be aloof to the fact that our actions might be a temptation to others? Absolutely not!

In addition to the Bible verses I supplied above, we can easily go broader. The greatest commandments are to love God and to love others. If we are knowingly leading others to sin, that is not loving them well.

The apostle Paul said it this way: *"For though I am free from all men, I have made myself a slave to all, so that I may win more."* (1 Corinthians 9:19)

The ultimate goal of Paul's life was to glorify God and to bring others to Christ. Our lives should look the same: free, but disciplined in our ultimate goal, fueled with a refusal of anything that compromises that goal.

And it all goes back to the heart, not the body.

#P31Prayer

God, this instruction is so much bigger than modesty. When we think about boiling down our lives to the two goals of You getting glory and others coming to know Christ, it magnifies our real purpose here. Help us to rid our lives of anything that distracts us from Your purposes. Expose any areas of our lives where we need correction. God, perform surgery on our hearts. Align them with Yours. Your Word is clear that if we seek first Your Kingdom and Your righteousness that You will add everything else to us *(Matthew 6:33)*. When we seek Your best, we get the rest. But when we get those purposes out of order, it all gets fuzzy. Your message is too important to risk its clarity. Help us to lay down our own agendas, our own selfishness and our own pride in order to pursue Your purposes more than our own. And God, we know that when our hearts are right with You, that You can order all the details that are less clear to us. Guide us in our decisions, and mold us into clear reflections of You. Forgive us for when we've sought our own glory. Thank you for Your grace. We love you. Amen.

#P31Practice

What is your heart's bend toward modesty? When you hear the word, are you filled with dread, dwelling on frumpy images, or are you up for the challenge of ensuring something as silly as a fashion choice doesn't rob God of His glory or compromise anyone else's walk with Christ?

His purposes must always trump our purposes. We are like a mist *(James 4:14)*, but He is forever *(Psalm 48:14)*. If our actions reflect anything different than this truth, we have elevated our own importance to a place that it never belongs.

I'm not going to challenge you to clean out your closet. (Although, if the Spirit prompts you, go for it!) But I am going to challenge you to search your heart. The Lord has worked on me so much in this area. I wish I could tell you that I'd never gotten this one wrong, but I know that many times I have.

As a reminder, take a dry erase marker, and simply write this on your mirror to remind you every day that:

His Purpose > My Freedom.

What God is teaching me about modesty:

day nineteen

#P31Goal

I plan ahead so that I do not have to neglect myself in the midst of providing for my family and serving others.

#P31Authority

She ***makes coverings for herself;*** *her clothing is* ***fine linen and purple.*** Proverbs 31:22

#P31Encouragement

On Day 12, we covered the idea that to best take care of them, we must also take care of ourselves. But let's be honest: the line between sacrifice and selfishness doesn't always seem crystal clear.

Thankfully, we get some help here. In verse 21, we see that

she makes clothing for her family. Here, we see that she makes clothing for herself.

Family is still first, but she does not neglect her own needs. Maybe you find yourself asking, *"But where does she find the time?"*

I think deep down, we know the answer. She doesn't have the time. She *makes* the time.

Remember that "whatever it takes" attitude? The attitude that is willing to rise while it is still night or not let the lamp go out at night? As if that isn't enough, we can see the "how" in verse 21, too. She has no fear of the snow for her household because her priority-planning prepared her.

The same principle of planning applies here. She's not selfishly putting her needs before the needs of others. But by planning ahead, she has allowed time to care for herself.

In my house, we joke that no one wants to be around Mommy until she's been with Jesus. (Or maybe we just joke that it's a joke, but it's really a fact!) But I know that if I don't prioritize getting up early, my day will get high-jacked before I've had any "me time," which includes time in my Bible and prayer with a cup of coffee, a workout 4-5 days of the week, and some days (not being more numerically specific than that), even a shower.

My husband I also carve out "me time" with date nights. With young kids, we often do date-nights at home or find ourselves benefitting from the early-bird special so we can be home in time to tuck our kids in bed, but I treasure those dates with him.

It's not super glamorous, but my girlfriends and I often catch up over coffee at Chick-Fil-A. I've even had groups of friends meet me at my house for 5:30am workouts. We all want to work-out, and we want to be together...but we have to be back home to help pack lunches and care for the younger ones before our husbands head to work.

Get the picture? "Me time" doesn't happen without intention and planning. Some seasons require more diligence and fancy footwork than others. But the work is worth it.

Maybe time isn't the issue for you, but you're curious about the attention to appearance, especially after yesterday's thoughts on modesty. Fine linen indicates her clothing was of good quality.

Purple, being the color of royalty, means that she does give attention to her own appearance.

It's just not excessive attention.

1 Peter 3:3-4 instructs, "*Your adornment must not be merely external - braiding the hair, and wearing gold jewelry or putting on dresses; but let it be the hidden person of the heart, with the imperishable quality of a gentle and quiet spirit, which is precious in the sight of God.*"

Our beauty is to radiate from the inside out, but it doesn't mean that we are called to completely neglect our appearance or caring for ourselves.

Looks just can't be the first thing on our priority list, and it shouldn't be the only good thing people have to say about us.

I know the pursuit of external beauty that is absent of inner beauty. It's an empty and meaningless road that leads to destruction. As I briefly mentioned on Day 12, I struggled with an eating disorder that quite honestly, should have claimed my life.

But anorexia wasn't the root of the real problem. My eating disorder was really just a symptom of the disease I was fighting in my heart. I was enslaved to sin instead of being controlled by righteousness *(Romans 6:18)*.[11]

So yes, let's plan ahead to have time to care for ourselves as we prioritize caring for our family and others. But above that, let's seek to please God with our hearts more than we seek to please anyone else with our appearance.

#P31Prayer

God, we confess that motherhood is often messy. It's easy to get distracted in the daily grind and to completely miss you in the process. But God, help us not to allow ourselves to be so unintentional that we become blind to the ways that you provide for us to care for ourselves. Don't let us believe the lie that we are to neglect ourselves as we care for others, but help us to find creative

---

[11] Myers, Michelle. *The Look that Kills: An Anorexic's Addition to Control*

ways to care for ourselves spiritually, emotionally, mentally and physically. Remind us not to wait to find the time, but to intentionally work to make the time. But God, align our priorities so that You get the honor and glory for our lives. Don't let us give excessive attention to the things that don't matter. Help our beauty radiate from the inside. Your Word reminds us that You are the strength of our hearts *(Psalm 73:26)*. Thank you for Your presence there. Make us beautiful in Your eyes, and captivate our focus toward pursuing inner beauty. Consistently remind us which beauty lasts. We love you. Amen!

#P31Practice

For me, working out tends to be the area of self-care where I have proven that I am capable of giving excessive attention. What area is it for you?

Maybe it's fixing your hair or make-up. Maybe it's shopping or just keeping up with the latest fashion trends. Again, there's nothing wrong with having interests in these areas, as long as we keep them in check.

Here's my check for myself: I refuse to give more time to exercise than I give to studying God's Word and in prayer. My body does not need more of my discipline than my heart does. As Paul wrote to Timothy, *"For physical training is of some value, but godliness has value for all things, holding promise for both the present life and the life to come"* (1 Timothy 4:8).

What boundary do you need to make for your life? Pray about it, and put it into practice. You won't regret it!

What boundaries do I need to put in place to ensure I take care of myself without crossing over to selfishness?

day twenty

#P31Truthbomb

I am an asset to my husband's life.

#P31Authority

Her husband is known** in the gates,* ***when he sits among the elders *of the land.* Proverbs 31:23

#P31Encouragement

We've gotten to know this woman's heart quite intimately over the last 19 days. In the next few days, we're going to get a peek into a few more of her admirable qualities and talents.

But today, we're shifting gears a bit to learn about her husband. And it turns out, knowing things about him also reveals quite a bit to us about her.

During Bible times, the gates were the center of civic and economic life. This verse lets us know that she isn't the only leader in her home; she married a leader, too.

One of my favorite things that I've ever heard my pastor say is that Ephesians 5 will look different in every home. That passage doesn't say that the wife can't have a career outside of the home, or that the man must make more money or climb the corporate ladder faster than the woman, etc. Any of those things that we try to squeeze in there are adding to the text.

But just as we've covered that the woman must diligently work at home, we see the clear expectation of the man: He's not sitting at home, doing nothing.

Don't worry; I'm not a man-hater. And this book isn't written to men, it's written to women. So what does all of this have to do with us? I've got a few ideas:

- ***Who we are doesn't hold our husbands back.***

His work matters. His talent matters.

We cannot become so consumed with our agenda that our spouses get left in the dust behind us. There's a popular book among female entrepreneurs that gives "advice" such as becoming your own idol and that the only way to support a revolution is to create your own. Basically, it shoots down any idea of teamwork and belittles the idea of offering support to anyone other than yourself.

Sweet friend, that kind of counsel is like cancer to your marriage...or any relationship that you care about for that matter. It doesn't matter how successful you are, how much money you make, or how much influence you have.

If you believe that you are more important than your spouse, or that your talents are better than his, expect rifts to develop in your relationship.

But this isn't limited to a business card. Do we have any personal fears or insecurities that are holding him back from reaching his full potential?

Maybe he was offered a new position, but we threw our foot

down saying that we refuse to uproot our family to move to a new city. Maybe God has laid a dream-business on his heart that he has to pursue outside of the job he works in order to provide for the family, but rather than encouraging him or offering our support, we nag him about every second that we don't have his attention.

Whatever this means for us, let's ensure that there's nothing in us that holds our husbands back from being the men that God has called them to be.

• ***Who we are enhances his reputation and influence.***

We slightly hit on this in Day 4, but let's dig a little deeper. Whatever we do should only increase our husband's success. Our integrity, our reputation, and our influence should only increase who he is to others.

Whether we realize it or not, each of our actions has a direct impact on how others will view our spouses.

Imagine this: You meet a woman at church. She is bubbly and fun. She's easy to talk to, and you find yourself feeling like you've known her for years. You're excited to find out that she has kids around the same age as yours, so without hesitation, you offer a dinner invitation for their entire family that next week.

You're so exited for dinner, and the night finally arrives. Your potential new BFF comes in, just as wonderful as she was on Sunday...but you quickly observe that her husband is less than pleasant. In fact, he's kind of a jerk.

Somewhere inside of you, a seed of doubt is planted in your mind: *What kind of crazy is she hiding behind this amazing front?*

Now, I'm not condoning judgment or saying that such a perception is accurate, but it's a reality of human interaction. The women we are will directly affect how others perceive our husbands.

Let's make sure that who we are only enhances his credibility.

• ***What if I'm still single?***

You are looking for a man of integrity who is capable of leading you. Not just to provide for you. But to truly lead you. And he is unqualified to lead you in the right direction if he is not following

Christ.

I'm not trying to be insensitive. I'm sure he's handsome. I know there has to be a lot of history between you. He's probably even a really nice guy.

But if he doesn't love Jesus even more than he loves you, there's no reason out there that's great enough for you to stay in a relationship that is less than God's best for you.

Paul wrote, *"Don't team up with those who are unbelievers. How can righteousness be a partner with wickedness? How can light live with darkness?"* (2 Corinthians 6:14) Now, this doesn't mean we shouldn't associate with unbelievers. (And this doesn't refer to those who are already in a marriage relationship with an unbeliever – we are going there next!)

But it does mean that we shouldn't interlock our personal lives closely with someone who might cause us to divide our loyalty between them and God.

I can't make a lot of promises, but I can promise you this: If you knowingly enter a marriage relationship with a spouse who does not know God, you have a lot of heartache ahead of you.

Can you imagine the daily agony of knowing the person you care about the most will be separated from God in eternity if they don't turn from their ways? Would you not hold your breath every time they walked out the door, praying, "Please, Jesus. Not yet. He's not ready."

I'm not exaggerating. I talk to too many women regularly who live this as their daily lives Love him enough to tell him the truth, and love God enough to obey His Word, even when you don't understand and it hurts.

Never settle for less than His best. He's proven Himself over and over again. His best is worth the wait. His best is better than what we are capable of asking or imagining. Trust Him.

• ***What if I'm married to an unbeliever?***

I think 1 Peter 3:1-2 might be one of the hardest things to apply in God's Word: *"Likewise, wives, be subject to your own husbands, so that even if some do not obey the Word, they may be won without a word by the conduct of their wives, when they see your respectful and pure conduct.*"

Without. A. Word. I want to face palm just thinking about it.

But if we're honest, even those of us with believing husbands know that the quickest way to promote resistance within our husbands is by resorting to nagging.

This isn't an exhaustive list, but here are two pieces of advice that I have for women in this position:

> ***Pray your guts out:*** When he puts up walls about your faith, ***pray.*** If he mocks your commitment to Christ, ***pray.*** If he shows any interest or steps in the right direction, ***pray.*** If he is completely silent and pretends there's no issue at all, ***pray.*** Prayer is not being silent. Prayer is a transfer of power from your need to God's hands. Release your husband over to God over and over again. Don't hold onto him with a death grip. With God, He's in much better hands. Can I promise you that your prayer will yield the result that you're after? No. I wish I could. But I can promise you that the time in prayer will change you. God provides peace that this world is incapable of understanding, and His peace will guard our hearts and minds in Jesus" *(Philippiana 4:7).* So if prayer changes us, we can't just pray for him. We have to pray for our witness to him, which is no small task.

> ***Be Jesus in front of Him:*** When we're treated with disrespect, the natural human response is disrespect. It's natural to treat others how they treat us. But it's *supernatural* to treat others how God has treated us. Jesus healed the ear of a soldier who came to arrest Him. From the cross, Jesus forgave His murderers. And while we were still sinners, God demonstrated His love for us with Christ's death *(Romans 5:8).* Be the best example of God's love that is possible. The more your behavior reflects Christ, the better

your chances at peaking your husband's curiosity and proving the authenticity of your belief.

Persevere, sister. It's hard, but the reward is great.

#P31Prayer

God, we thank you for writing our love stories. Whether we have a fairytale romance, a story that has yet to be told, or a relationship where we are begging you to show up and be a part of, we trust You. God, help us to be assets to our husbands. Help us to prioritize being their biggest supporters. May everything that we do add to his credibility and success. If there is anything in us that would make others think less than him, strip it from us. We don't want to hold him back in any way from the plans that You have for him. Give us the discernment to see Your great purposes at work in our lives. For the single women, I pray for patience to wait for Your best. I pray that they wouldn't settle or compromise, but that they would wait for a man of Your standard. For the women married to unbelievers, I pray that You would help them be dedicated to prayer. God, my not knowing her exact situation doesn't matter, because You know all things. Give her the strength to be Jesus right in front of him. Soften his heart, Lord. Work in him. Make Yourself known to him in a way that he will know is You. Through it all, Lord, no matter our circumstance, help us to remember that You are enough for us. Thank You for your superior goodness in all things. We love You. Amen.

#P31Practice

If you've picked up this book, I have no doubt you're a strong woman. It's rare that strength and support are taught hand-in-hand, but I believe that one of the strongest things we can do as wives is to be a strong support system for our husbands.

Here are 10 ideas of how we can best support the man that God has given us:

1. ***Pray about his relationship with God.***
   Whether he has a growing relationship with the Lord or not, prayer is the best place to begin to support our husbands. When we pray, we are taking our husbands to the largest Source of strength in existence.

2. ***Pray about his success and influence with others.***
   We have the opportunity to be our spouse's greatest support system and encourager. Do more than just *want* good things for Him; *pray* God will max out his influence for the Kingdom.

3. ***Praise Him in public.***
   It's so easy to find opportunities to criticize, especially when we want someone to be on "our side." But deny the temptation to belittle him to others and elevate him often. Even on the hardest days of marriage, we must cling to the good, and if we're willing to examine closely enough, we can always find something to be grateful for.

4. ***Praise Him in private.***
   Frequent praise prevents us from getting distracted by nit-picky preferences. Praise not only has the power to change his attitude, but it changes our heart in the process when we remind ourselves of all he does that is good.

   Why the distinction between public praise and private praise? Private praise promotes intimacy, but it also eliminates any perception of false motives. Praising him when no one else is around shows your commitment to simply build him up.

5. ***Thank him daily.***
   Yes, even if he does not reciprocate. Kindness will never steer us in the wrong direction.

6. ***Ask, "What's one thing I can do to help you today?"***
   This likely won't require a huge amount of time or effort. But isn't a quick errand or a prayer for him before an important meeting worth the huge investment you're making in the foundation of your marriage?

7. ***Spend 10 minutes in prayer for every one minute of criticism.***
   This one piece of advice from one of my mentors, Pat Cooper, drastically changed my marriage. I quickly realized, "if I'm not willing to dedicate 10 minutes to prayer, it's probably not even worth mentioning to James." Consider this tip an instant "nagging filter" for your marriage.

8. ***Let him lead.***
   Yes, there are plenty of things you can do for yourself. But most men want to lead. Whenever you get an opportunity to let him lead, take it. If you married him, he is worth following.

9. ***In arguments, be on the side of your marriage.***
   Commit that your marriage is more important than "winning" or being right. Lay pride aside, and be on the side of your marriage. The relationship takes priority over being right.

10. ***Be his safe place.***
    You should be the one place where your husband knows that he won't be shut down. Let him be real. Let him let his guard down. He shouldn't need to worry that if he lets his feelings show he is going to be subject to criticism.

How can I be a better asset to my husband's life?

day twenty-one

#P31Goal

I utilize the gifts God that has given me for the benefit of others.

#P31Authority

*She **makes linen garments and sells them,** and supplies belts to the tradesmen.* Proverbs 31:24

#P31Encouragement

Warning: my business nerd is going to show today. I just love the character discoveries that are in place for today.

Remember what we read in vs. 22? How she makes fine linen garments for herself? Today's takeaway shows us that she simply took her ability one step further by opening an avenue to provide for others with what has benefitted her own life.

Her business was built out of meeting her own needs and realizing that her gift could also be a blessing to those around her. Can we say "authenticity?" Her business isn't grounded in becoming popular or profitable. The foundation of her business is *purpose.*

Now, whether you open a business or not, God has unquestionably made you uniquely gifted. Here's our character revelation:

What talents and abilities has God given you that may be a blessing to others? And, how are you using those?

1 Peter 4:10-11 says, *"Each of you should use whatever gift you have received to serve others, as faithful stewards of God's grace in its various forms If anyone speaks, they should do so as one who speaks the very words of God. If anyone serves, they should do so with the strength God provides, so that in all things God may be praised through Jesus Christ. To him be the glory and the power for ever and ever. Amen."*

Let's dig a little deeper into these rich words:

• ***No gift God has given us is to go unused.***

We serve an intentional and purposeful God. If He gave you a talent, it wasn't because He was bored. He desires you to use it. Refusal to use our gifts, whether the result of stubbornness or laziness, we must see as disobedience. That's the bottom line: It's not "humility" to refuse to use the gift that God has given us. It's disobedience.

• ***The purpose of every gift is to benefit others.***

God also did not give us a gift, talent or ability purely for our own use or enjoyment. Because He gifted each of us uniquely, we are to use the gifts that He has given us to serve one another. Selfish use of our gifts isn't using our gifts up to God's standard. We're only using the gifts that He has given us effectively if we are using them to serve others.

• ***Refusing to use your gift is poor stewardship of God's grace.***

The NASB translation uses the phrase "manifold of God's grace," implying that by putting various gifts on display, our diversity of gifts brings unity to our common message of God's grace. Yes, God made us differently so we could be better together. But He also made us differently so that we could relate to different people, and simultaneously, reach more people in His name. The purpose doesn't end with the gift. The purpose always drives back to building relationships with others that provide opportunities to share God's message with them.

- ***Using your gift does not require your own ability.***

I always say that my seasons of writing are my most humbling seasons. Throughout writing this book, I've gotten so many reminders that this project is much more of a reflection what He has taught me than it is a display of my knowledge or me being a talented writer. He doesn't require us to be superstars. He just wants willing hearts and obedient spirits. Then, He can do the rest in us. If He's called you, friend, rest assured, He will also equip you.

- ***God gets the glory when we use our gifts.***

It's not about the worldly applause or the spotlight. It's about people being able to see Jesus at work in us and giving Him the praise. Jesus put it this way: "*Let your light shine before men so that they may see your good works and praise your Father in heaven*" (Matthew 5:16).

Our job is to make sure we that are giving credit where credit is due and keeping our hearts in the right place. We live in an "approval addicted" world. It's easy to get distracted, to get caught up in basking in the praise of others, and to be tempted to keep it for ourselves.

But we must remember, sisters: Whenever we receive glory but we do not deflect it back to God, we throw away the eternal reward. Whatever blessing we get is quick, cheap and inferior to His plan. Don't settle for the world's cheap knock-off; the Designer option is not far away!

We already chatted about money on Day 11 (feel free to go back and review!), but since most people don't equate selling with godliness, let me just make one final observation.

You don't have to feel guilty about operating a business that is rooted in purpose. If money or status is the end game, then there are some character issues to question. But if you remain the "purpose police" of your business and stay committed to pursue His mission with excellence, you can proceed with a clear conscience.

#P31Prayer

God, thank you for making each of us *on* purpose and *with* purpose. Thank You for making us differently. Help us to work together better so that we can reach more people effectively for Your Kingdom. Forgive us when we are stubborn or lazy. Forgive us when pride prevents us from being good teammates for our Christian brothers and sisters. Fill us with humility to accomplish Your purposes over any agenda of our own. Help us to use our gifts, not just for ourselves, but to serve others. Help us to remember that when we let our light shine, it's not so that we can be seen. Like C.S. Lewis wrote, it's so that others can see You. Don't let us settle for the world's version of Your approval that is so inferior to Yours. Give us the patience to pursue eternal blessing. Reveal to us how we can best use our lives to make the most of them for You. Give us the boldness and the courage. Thank You for equipping us for every good work. We love You. Amen.

#P31Practice

Are you struggling with figuring out what your gifts and abilities are? Here are some places in God's Word where you can go to get an idea of some of the "various gifts" that Peter wrote about in 1 Peter 4:

Romans 12:6-8
1 Corinthians 12:8-11
Ephesians 4:11

That's not an exhaustive list, but it's a good place to begin to get your wheels turning as you pray for God to provide opportunities to bring Him glory.

But here's my encouragement for you: Think outside the box. Sometimes, our gifts are the things that come the most naturally to us. Like the P31 woman, it's the things that we do for ourselves that become second nature.

But other times, gifts are really unexpected blessings. It's the journey that God takes us on where we learn lessons that will be valuable for others. Perhaps it's even the thing that we think, "There's no way God could use me to do that."

His power is made perfect in weakness, sweet friend *(2 Corinthians 12:9)*. So, yes, He can!

It's a consistent thread in Scripture. God loves to use the underdog.

If this former anorexic can start a fitness ministry... If this fashion-challenged tomboy can run a clothing line... If this unnatural business brain can run a ministry for Christian women in business...

I have absolutely no doubt that He can richly use you. And if you respond in obedience, He absolutely will.

What are the gifts and abilities God has given me?

How can I use what God has given me to bring Him glory?

day twenty-two

#P31Goal

My work in business is done with a heart for ministry.

#P31Authority

She makes linen garments and sells them, and ***supplies belts to the tradesmen.*** Proverbs 31:24

#P31Encouragement

Yesterday, we chatted about utilizing our gifts with purpose in mind. Today, that purpose gets amplified because we're able to see that ministry isn't just something she talks about; it's something she does.

The first half of this verse talks about selling; but today, we're honing in on how she supplies belts to the tradesmen.

There's a big difference between selling and supplying. Selling is the exchange of goods for a profit. Supplying is providing for a missing need.

Supplying is ministry.

Businesses that are grounded in purpose sell to some, but supply *something* to all. This doesn't necessarily mean a tangible product.

I typically encourage business women I mentor that purpose-driven businesses are defined as "a business with a message so important that the message getting out to as many people as possible matters more than the money coming in."

What's your message? What benefit can people encounter from your business, whether they actually decide to do business with you or not?

Michelle, are you sure it's ministry? I mean, she's just giving them a belt.

Yes! The word "tradesmen" originates from the word *Canaanites* in Hebrew. Their being tradesmen does mean they were masters of trade, but it also lets us know they were not followers of the God of Israel.

By supplying them with a belt, she had the opportunity to interact with people who were not following God. The belt was a doorway to enter into a relationship with them. And just maybe, if they liked her belt, if they were able to strike up a conversation, if they were able to become friends...she would get an opportunity to share about her God with them.

That belt was building her credibility with them. Her starting point was to meet a physical need, but her hope that was that she would someday get the opportunity to minister to a spiritual need.

That belt was definitely ministry!

Maybe you're thinking, "I don't have a business. Do I need one?" We're covering it here because it's mentioned, but you don't have to have a business to be able to do ministry.

Here are three questions we can all answer:

• ***What do you do in your life that gives you opportunities to share the gospel with those who don't know God?***
If we allow ourselves to get distracted, it's easy to forget the urgency of our message. To forget the desperation in our lives before we found our purpose in Christ.

We forget the large number of people that we see every single day that are spiritually sick, and that we have the only antidote.

I'll confess: When you look at the dedication of the evil forces in our world, does it make you angry like it does me? We have terrorists with malicious agendas. They're wrong, and yet, they recruit with intense vigor.

If we're honest, we will admit they recruit with more passion than we share our faith. And *we're* the ones on the winning team.

There's something seriously wrong with that picture!

In Luke 10:1-22, Jesus offers a charge to new believers who were going out in His name to spread God's message. These were not trained theologians. These were not seasoned Christians.

These were new believers whose lives had been changed by God.

You don't have to know every spiritual doctrine in existence before you can lead someone to Christ. You just have to know that because God loved us so much, He sent His Son, Jesus, to die in our place. And if we believe in Him, we gain eternal acceptance from God *(John 3:16)*. If we choose not to believe in Jesus, we will experience God's eternal wrath for our rejection of His gift to all *(John 3:36)*.

Our willingness to share this truth could mean the difference between someone experiencing God's eternal acceptance or God's eternal wrath.

We cannot be ashamed of this message. God's intention in sending Jesus was never to condemn, but to save *(John 3:17)*. It's literally the best offer we will ever have the opportunity to present to someone!

• ***What ways are you using the influence you have been given to***

minister to the needs around you?

Sometimes, that word "influence" intimidates people. They think, "I don't have influence. I'm just a [*fill in the blank with your excuse or fear.*]"

God didn't create any "*just a's.*" He has put you in the exact position where you are for a particular purpose. Just as Mordecai charged Esther, *"And who knows but that you can come to your royal position for such a time as this?"* (Esther 4:14b).

Your position might not be considered a royal one, but it's still a valuable one! God has given no one else the exact seat He has given you. No one else has the same sphere of influence.

I have no doubt that you are the greatest influence on at least one person's life. I have no doubt that you are the strongest believer, *if not the only believer,* someone in your life knows. I'm sure that there are many people in your life who care enough to listen to you and desire your input on their life decisions.

You have influence. We all do. It's just up to us to put it to good use.

• ***Does my purpose contribute to His purpose?***

Jesus said, *"The harvest is plentiful, but the workers are few. Ask the Lord of the harvest, therefore, to send out workers into his harvest field"* (Luke 10:2).

Basically, this was Jesus' reminder to us that there are more people who need this message than there are those who are willing to tell it. Being ministry-minded in our life means that we are consistently living with an eternal perspective. We remain focused on the main goal.

Yes, He's given each of us a unique purpose. But the greatest purpose that we can ever be a part of is His ultimate purpose of bringing people into a saving relationship with Jesus Christ.

Our purpose is not separate from His purpose. Our purpose should feed into and be wrapped up in His purpose. And if we're spending more time praying about our purpose than His purpose, our life requires an alignment check.

#P31Prayer

God, give me a heart that pursues You above all. Take the driven aspects of my personality and channel my efforts for Your glory, not my own. Open my eyes to see opportunities to build relationships with those who don't know You. Help me to use my gifts to serve them, not so they would think more of me, but so they would think more of You. Open doors for me to continue to cultivate those relationships. But God, more than just my actions, provide a way for me to share Your truth openly and bring them into a saving relationship with You. Oh God, bigger than our influence, we pray that you would send us *more*. Make *more* believers bold enough to stand in the gap for Your name. We know there are many who don't know you, and none of us can undertake this task alone. But if we have more who work together, rather than wasting our energy on dividing among those who believe in You, we could have a much greater impact together. Help us to lay aside egos, preferences, or anything else that could get in the way of Your truth. Your purposes and Your agenda trump ours every single time. Use us, Lord. We are here, and we are willing. We love you. Amen.

#P31Practice

I'm not going to pretend that sharing our faith doesn't require us to step outside of our comfort zones. But God doesn't call us to be comfortable. He calls us to be bold and courageous. And we're not exactly splitting hairs here. Our message determines where people spent eternity.

Today, let's pray for opportunities to be bold witnesses for Him. Let's pray that He will put people in our path who desperately need Him in their lives.

Here are some important things for us to remember when we share our faith:

• ***We are just the messenger, not the Savior.***
God saves them, not us. We can remove the pressure from ourselves. Our only responsibility is to share Jesus. God is the one who captures hearts and saves souls.

• ***If they reject the message, they are rejecting God, not us.***
We don't need to fear rejection. If they choose to say "no" to Christ's message, they are truly rejecting Him *(Luke 10:16)*. This doesn't mean that we won't hurt for them afterwards. When we know someone has a hardened heart toward God, it will make our hearts feel heavy. But if we have done our job in communicating the truth of His message, in that situation, our heart may be heavy, but our hands will be clean.

• ***Expect opposition.***
When we actively share our faith, we move ourselves to the frontlines of spiritual warfare. In fact, isn't it crazy that when Paul was attempting to re-establish his credibility after the Corinthians were wooed by false teachers, he didn't use all of his accomplishments? Instead, he recounted all of the hardships that he endured in spreading Christ's message *(2 Corinthians 11:23-29)*.

But let's stay focused and remember what is ahead. Wouldn't you rather have a hard life than an empty one?

My prayer for boldness in sharing my faith:

"I'd rather have a hard life than an empty one." Michelle Myers

day twenty-three

#P31Goal

I am a woman of discipline and dignity.

#P31Authority

***Strength** and **dignity** are her clothing; and she smiles at the future.*
Proverbs 31:25

#P31Encouragement

This woman makes clothes for a living, and her character is so strong that her clothing is listed as strength and dignity. Don't you love it? That's such a powerful word picture. These traits are so evident in her life that it's as if you can physically see them. They wrap up and put the finishing touches on who she is as a woman.

Are they displayed that boldly in our lives? Let's find out.

• ***Discipline***

Strength, whether it is physical, mental, emotional or spiritual, is the result of discipline. Physical strength requires disciplined efforts to increase our muscles' capacity for work. Mental strength requires intense focus. Emotional strength requires that we remain calm in our actions, despite circumstance. Spiritual strength comes from a strong reliance on the Lord, rooted in time spend with Him in prayer and in His Word.

Bottom line: Strength does not just appear. Strength is the result of discipline.

So to clear up the confusion, let's see "strength" here as "disciplined." Rather than focusing on the result, let's keep the emphasis on the effort that produces the right result.

Here's a definition I've heard of discipline that has stuck with me: *"Discipline is choosing what I want* ***most*** *instead of what I want* ***now.****"*

In the different areas of our life, do we choose what we want most more than what we want now?

> *If we get into an argument with our spouse, do we choose prioritizing our marriage over being right?*
>
> *In that interaction with the non-believer who treats us poorly, do we choose kindness so they can see Christ in us, or do we lash back with similar hatred?*
>
> *When our alarm goes off in the morning to have our devotional time before the day begins, do we choose to get out of bed and spend time with Him, or do we hit the snooze button?*

Making the disciplined choice is often not the most fun option. In fact, Hebrews 12:11 goes so far as telling us that no discipline is pleasant, but instead is painful in the moment. But discipline brings a "peaceful harvest of right living" *(Hebrews 12:11).*

Discipline ultimately brings peace. If we are patient and able to delay instant gratification for long-term reward, we will have peace in our hearts.

And if we don't have discipline, we are faced with the opposite of peace: Tension. Stress. Worry. Restlessness. Anxiety.

Discipline is often the first step to curing that unsettled feeling in our soul.

In the last few years, I've realized that I have to let discipline and passion work together. Most of us tend to lean toward one or the other. Passion is awesome. It's such a beautiful thing. But passion means that we let our emotions mark our paths.

Just being real? Feelings make a terrible compass for life!

For example, when my alarm goes off, I rarely desire to leave my cozy haven of the warm covers. But in the moments that I allow discipline to be the catalyst to be what gets me started, I find that passion eventually shows up and can take over. The alarm goes off, discipline gets me out of bed, I began reading His Word, He begins to speak truth into my life, and then I'm fired up and so grateful I got out of bed.

But if we wait on passion to be there first, we'll find ourselves letting our emotions guide the areas of our lives that can't thrive with a compass that's often defective.

Discipline: our catalyst for passion, the key to strength, and refusing to settle for what we want temporarily for what we want ultimately.

• ***Dignity***

In short, she is worthy of respect.

I would argue that everyone wants respect, but it's a much smaller percentage that are willing to do the work required to earn it.

Ready for the respect recipe?

1 Thessalonians 4:11-12 tells us to *"make it your ambition to lead a quiet life: You should mind your own business and work with your hands, just as we told you,* ***so that your daily life may win the respect of outsiders..."***

Let's dissect his advice by phrase:

• ***"Make it your ambition..."***
This is a goal. Goals are not things that happen by accident; they are dreams with deadlines. Ambition seems to have gotten a bit of a bad reputation among Christian circles, but goals are definitely a part of the Christian life. Selfish goals, not so much. But if our goals align with His goals, we're doing our part to ensure we are not living an aimless life.

• ***"...to lead a quiet life"***
Thankfully, this doesn't mean quiet in the sense of volume. *(And all the extroverts said, "Amen!")* Rather, it's to live peaceably among others. Basically, it's the reminder that we are to choose our battles wisely. As Paul would later write to Timothy, the only fight worth fighting is the good fight of the faith *(2 Timothy 4:7).*

There are many ways I could dive into this here. Let's start by agreeing that frequent issues will probably arise with nonbelievers because people act out what they believe. If we expect people who don't know Jesus to act with our same moral compass, we will find ourselves frequently frustrated. Expect it, embrace it, and in all but "good fight issues," turn all the cheeks you have...and then turn them again *(Matthew 5:39).*

But let's talk about how many silly arguments break out among believers. Do we realize that those nit-picky, silly, childish issues that we argue over makes us look just like the world? I'm pretty sure God's Word provides the exact opposite instruction *(Romans 12:2).*

Preaching to myself here: That's a pretty steep price to pay just to be right.

We're on the same team. Let's make sure we act like it.

• ***"You should mind your own business..."***
Oh, social media. It was a problem before, but you certainly have made this "easier" for us to be able to poke our noses

where they don't belong and provide our opinions when they're not needed. There's so much chatter available to us. We live in noisy times.

Have you ever been to a track meet? If a runner steps outside of their lane in the race, you'll hear a loud siren and a judge offer them the "Disqualified" sign. No matter how fast they were going or what position they were, if they step outside of their lane, they are ineligible to win.

The Christian life may not come with blow horns when we step outside of what is considered to be "our business," but we certainly have the Holy Spirit inside of us to help us have discernment. Listen to His still, small voice inside of you when you question whether or not you should get involved in a situation.

One of our favorite pastor friends, Stuart Henslee put it this way, "God has called you to reflect His glory in your life. You don't have time for most things."

Let's stay in our lanes.

- ***"and work with your hands..."***

Thessalonica was a city mixed with Greeks and Romans. These were the two leading cultures. Their respected leaders were hard-working, high-impact, successful people. So, in order to be respected by them, having a strong work ethic was required.

God is clear in His Word that we are to work hard at whatever we do *(Ecclesiastes 9:10)*. We're to work with the idea that God is our direct supervisor *(Colossians 3:23)*.

Whether we realize it or not, our work ethic is a powerful part of our witness. Let's make sure we work in such a way that others have the opportunity to see Jesus.

Despise your current job? *Choose joy anyway.*

Extremely successful in your career that you love? *Give all the glory you receive back to God where it belongs.*

The task doesn't matter. The paycheck doesn't matter. But our effort does.

• ***"so that your daily life may win the respect of outsiders..."*** The Thessalonians were living among many nonbelievers. Paul's instructions here were guiding them on how to be able to gain the respect of others who believe differently than they did.

Bottom line: if someone doesn't respect you, there's no way they will listen to you. Paul's instruction was breaking down the steps they needed to take so that they could earn the respect of nonbelievers in their city in order to open doors for sharing the gospel.

No matter what, we have to keep the main thing the main thing. Our consistency in living boldly in the way of Christ matters so much more than our preference or personal comfort.

Think about the very title of this book. We won't be famous in heaven if we aren't bringing people with us.

#P31Prayer

God, clothe us with strength and dignity. Help us to live our lives with Your purpose in mind. Help us to choose to be disciplined and to trust that, as we are making choices that honor You, our passion will show up. Discipline may feel like the boring choice in the moment, but God, we know that walking with You is the greatest adventure we could ever be a part of. Don't let us cut ourselves short for selfishness and miss out on Your best for us. Help us to remember that as we draw near to You that You will draw near to us. Also, Lord, help us to live in such a way that earns respect from those around us. Help us to patiently pursue peace as much as possible. Help us to lay down our prideful defenses often and only pick up Your armor to fight the good fight. Provide opportunities for the ordinary ways in which we live our daily lives to open up extraordinary miracles that make You known. It's not about us, Lord, but about You. Make our lives reflect that truth. Thank You for the opportunity to represent You. May we always remember that great responsibility even in the smallest parts of our day. We love you. Amen.

#P31Practice

Today is going to be a tough one. Let's bless a difficult person in our lives.

Whether the person claims Christ or is far from Him, we all have at least one unavoidable difficult relationship in our lives. The normal response to these people is to either treat them how they treat us or to play by the *Bambi* rule of ignoring them if we can't find something nice to say.

But we do have another option: choosing kindness. Extraordinary, unexplainable, unmerited kindness.

Can you think of a better representation of God's grace toward us?

Most people soften with kindness. Not all, but most. But regardless of their response, you will be able to embrace the reality that you made the God-honoring choice.

> *If your enemies are hungry, give them food to eat. If they are thirsty, give them water to drink. You will heap burning coals of shame on their heads, and the Lord will reward you.* Proverbs 25:21-22

Kindness is how God calls us to retaliate against our enemies. Total transparency? In the moments that I do choose kindness, I may or may not imagine those burning coals over their head.

Go above and beyond for that person today. You just might have the pleasure of watching God move in a way that you didn't know was possible.

Who is God calling me to retaliate against with His kindness? What is He asking me to do?

day twenty-four

#P31Goal

I have joyful confidence in my God and His plan for me.

#P31Authority

Strength and dignity are her clothing; and she ***smiles at the future.*** Proverbs 31:25

#P31Encouragement

Truth: Smiling is more effective for adding to your beauty than any designer make-up. But smiling it not just about being attractive on the outside, it's a reflection of the joy that radiates inside of us.

Debbie-downer. Sourpuss. Constant complainer. Whatever

you want to call it, if those are traits people could use to describe us, we're not an accurate depiction of our God. No one is attracted to or inspired by negativity, stress, and worry.

This isn't fake or naïve positivity. The reason why we can smile at our future is rooted in two things:

• ***Our confidence is in God, not ourselves.***

I love the encouragement in Philippians 4:13, *"I can do all things through Christ who strengthens me!"* But we often miss out the true power in these words if we miss the two verses just before this often-quoted phrase:

> *I am not saying this because I am in need, for I have learned to be content whatever the circumstances. I know what it is to be in need, and I know what it is to have plenty. I have learned the secret of being content in any and every situation, whether well fed or hungry, whether living in plenty or want.* Philippians 4:11-12

Isn't Paul's confidence in God mind-blowing? I doubt many of us have actually experienced true hunger. But Paul had, and it hadn't shaken His confidence in God. Most of us live with all of our needs and a good portion of our wants. Paul had lived truly in need. But His confidence in God remained strong.

Contentment in Christ is the only way we will ever put our full confidence in Him. The little seeds of discontentment that we see pop up in our lives truly reveal the areas of our hearts we haven't fully committed to Him.

Discontent with your current level of influence? That might be selfish ambition.

Discontent with your finances? That might indicate a little too much emphasis on money.

Our strength to overcome our struggle is unleashed the moment we decide to be content with where God has us now.

I'll admit – I've struggled with this in the past. I think somehow that I had contentment and complacency confused. God has called us to contentment, but not to complacency, so what's the difference?

> *But godliness with contetment is great gain.* 1 Timothy 6:6

When our contentment is rooted in godliness, honoring God stays anchors our focus. Not only does His purpose trump our preference, but He is simultaneously established as our measuring stick.

That's right. These seven powerful words not only kill complacency and elevate contentment, but they shatter thoughts of comparison. We simply pursue Him and His best for us, rather than trying to keep up with or measure up to anyone else.

Let's just take a second, and let that truth soak in: He is enough.

We very much live in a "Jesus and" world. One that says, "I love Jesus as long as He...." Or "I will always choose Jesus, unless He makes me choose between Him and..."

If we aren't careful, it's easy to slip into "conditional Christianity," which to be honest, isn't Christianity at all.

James 1:4 says to let our *"steadfastness have its full effect, that you have be perfect and complete, lacking in nothing."*

Perfect and complete doesn't mean that we never mess up or that we have it all figured out. It just means that no matter what circumstance we're in, Jesus truly is enough. He really is all we need.

And even if it's just Him that we have, we still have much to be grateful for. We unlock our fullness of confidence in Christ with contentment in Him only.

• ***We've done what we can do to be prepared.***

There are so many examples in Scripture where God required an action step of His servant before He intervened with His power.

Before God parted the Red Sea, He asked Moses to raise His staff and stretch His hand out over the waters *(Exodus 14:16).*

David had to actually go into a man-to-man (really boy-to-giant) battle against Goliath to defeat the great Philistine army *(1 Samuel 17).*

God instructed Elisha to ask Naaman to dip himself seven times in the Jordan River to be cured of His leprosy *(2 Kings 5).*

We often see Jesus doing the same thing. For example, He healed a lame man and instructed him to, *"Get up and walk"* (John 5:8).

God is our great Provider, but that doesn't mean that He doesn't require us to be an active participant in His mission. We respond as obediently as we can, and He does the rest.

Our P31 woman does such a good job of being a living example of this. She is disciplined, purposeful and prepared. She's taken full responsibility with her time, her talent and her resources, and she leaves the rest up to God.

May we walk this closely with Him, with such confidence in Him, not arrogance in ourselves. God is our only sure thing. Why would we put any confidence in an inferior source?

Let's build a relationship with Him that's so strong that it literally changes our countenance. Whatever our circumstance, let's smile at our future because we know that God is on our side, and He's enough.

#P31Prayer

God, we praise You for Your infinite wisdom and power in our lives. It's seriously so amazing that You have specific plans for each of us. You knitted us together carefully in our mother's wombs *(Psalm 139:13).* Your plans for us are rooted in Your hope and for our good *(Jeremiah 29:11).* We can trust You in everything and with everything. Thank You for being our sure thing. God, help us to pursue the difference between complacency and contentment. Call us to action, and help us to respond quickly in accordance to Your will. Help us put our full confidence in You and not to rely on ourselves. Help us to abandon our control-freak ways and to relinquish total control over our lives into Your powerful hands. Make us bold women of prayer who turn to prayer as our first response, not our last resort. Help us to be prepared for what we can, but to trust You beyond our preparedness. Let our resilience in trials make You bigger in the lives of others. Help us to choose joy despite circumstances and bask in the promise that You are enough for us. Thank You for being all we need and more than what we deserve. We are content in You, and we are confident in You. We love you. Amen.

#P31Practice

We can't address "smiling at the future" without addressing one of the biggest stumbling blocks to accomplishing that goal: worry.

Jesus asked, *"Can any of you, by worrying, add a single hour to your life?"* (Matthew 6:27)

Jesus is reminding us of a few things here. Worrying distracts us from our main purpose, keeps us from releasing full trust to God, and can even negatively effect our health.

But isn't worry a part of life? Even if we do what we can to be prepared, won't life always throw us curveballs we can't prepare for?

Yes. Certainly, circumstances will happen that will tempt us worry. But when those moments happen, we must turn our worries into prayers. Jesus plainly reminded us here that worrying is a waste of time. And we know that prayer is productive! We can't control all things, but we know the One who can!

If you're a frequent worrier, here are two tips that I have greatly helped me:

• ***Turn it over to God.***

Prayer is a transfer of our problems into God's power. If you're trying to handle something that you can't handle, there's a reason you are overwhelmed. You're in over your head. Prayer may not change our circumstance, but it certainly has the power to change us in the process.

Often, we do this too late. We do everything in our power to "fix it," and when all of our attempts fail, we turn to God as a last resort. Sweet friend, we will save ourselves a lot of time and heartache if we will go to God as our first response. He's the

Fixer, not us.

• ***To trust Him more, increase your time with Him.*** Consistently trying to fix life's struggles on our own literally means we have a white-knuckle death-grip on our problems. Why do we delude ourselves into thinking we are more trustworthy than God to solve our situation?

Trust with God is built just like any other relationship. The more time we spend in His Word, getting to know His character and how He has acted over time, the more time we spend worshipping Him, the more time we spend in conversation with Him, the more we talk with others about Him who are seeking Him, the more we will trust Him.

The more we will be okay with Him not doing things the way we want because we know His way never fails.

The more we can remain calm even when we don't understand because we know His understanding is so much greater than ours will ever be.

The more we will be completely be at peace with whatever outcome He decides.

The more time we spend with Him, the more confident we will become because, as we see how He keeps His promises over and over again in His Word, we will also see Him keeping His promises over and over again in our lives.

Need to turn a worry into a prayer? Take that extra time today, and release that burden over to the One who can carry it effortlessly.

My Worries	*My Prayers*

day twenty-five

#P31Goal

I know when to speak with wisdom and when expressing my opinion is not necessary.

#P31Authority

She ***opens her mouth in wisdom,*** *and the teaching of kindness is on her tongue.* Proverbs 31:26

#P31Encouragement

If we're honest, opening our mouths is not the challenge. It's making sure that we open our mouths only when we have wisdom to share. And then there's the even harder part: If we know when to open our mouths, this also implies that we know when to keep our mouths shut.

Before we dig into the discernment of when to open our mouths and when to close them, let's first make sure we understand the difference between wisdom and knowledge. Knowledge is merely a collection of facts, but wisdom is the ability to apply what we know to our lives.

It sounds more difficult than it actually is. For example, Proverbs 9:10 reminds us that *"the fear of the Lord is the beginning of wisdom."* Knowledge reminds us that He is our Creator. But wisdom reminds us that as the Creator of our lives, He has the most insight on how we should live.

It gets even more simple. How do we get this wisdom? We just need to ask.

> *If any of you lacks wisdom, you should ask God, who gives generously to all without finding fault, and it will be given to you.* James 1:5

God doesn't withhold wisdom from His children who are actively seeking Him. In fact, "*His divine power has given us everything we need for a godly life through our knowledge of Him who called us by his own glory and goodness.*" (2 Peter 1:3)

Notice, I used the word "simple" and avoided "easy." Easy implies effortless, while simple, while not challenging, still requires discipline.

It's the discernment part that gets tricky. Here are five truths from God's Word to help us determine situations where we should speak or remain quiet.

• ***Don't major on minor issues.*** *"Flee the evil desires of youth and pursue righteousness, faith, love and peace, along with those who call on the Lord out of a pure heart. Don't have anything to do with foolish and stupid arguments, because you know they produce quarrels."* (2 Timothy 2:22-23)

How much "free time" do you think the P31 woman has? She is so intentional, remembering that each moment she lives impacts her legacy. Gossip and silly arguments aren't an issue because she doesn't make time for things that don't matter. She's focused on God's ultimate agenda and what He has specifically asked her to do.

How we spend our time is a big indicator of our character. Words are easy to say and behavior can be manipulated, but what we spend most of our time doing says a lot about who we really are.

• ***Dealing with the sins of others is to be done privately and for the sole purpose of restoration.*** *"If your brother sins against you, go and tell him his fault, between you and him alone. If he listens to you, you have gained your brother."* (Matthew 18:15)

Even if we feel someone is making a poor moral decision, deciding to publicly shame them to inflate our own egos is every bit as sinful as whatever action they have committed.

Because of God's instruction in Scripture, the number of people whose sins we should comment on, if at all, is limited to people we know personally. If there's someone we don't know personally, we should stay in our lane by keeping our audible mouths shut. If we are genuinely burdened for someone we do not have a personal relationship with, we should spend our energy praying that God would use someone in their life to speak the truth that they need in their life.

Many times, we need to remember the truth that sometimes, God wants our prayers more than He needs our voice. Speaking doesn't have the power to change hearts in itself, but prayer does.

This doesn't mean sin can't be addressed publicly. We should absolutely teach about the seriousness of sin. But it is possible to teach what God says about sin without shooting down the sinner. Sin is addressed publicly; sinners are addressed privately.

• ***It's impossible to humbly accept God's standard of grace for ourselves while pridefully holding others to a standard of perfection.*** *"For in the same way you judge others, you will be judged, and with the measure you use, it will be measured to you."* (Matthew 7:2)

Remember, God's grace doesn't just stop at mercy. I once heard my pastor, Bruce Frank, say that mercy is simply not getting what we deserve [hell], but grace takes it a step further and gives us what we don't deserve [heaven].

Maybe you're thinking, "I just don't have enough grace for all the mistakes being made in this twisted world."

Exactly. None of us do. Only God does. That's why the majority of the time, we need to release ourselves from most situations and allow God to deliver both the grace and the judgment at His discretion.

• ***Love is to be the underlying motive of everything we do.*** *"By this, all people will know that you are my disciples, if you have love for one another."* (John 13:35)

After six years of full-time public ministry, I doubt it surprises anyone that I receive criticism and push back. Expect spiritual warfare, right *(1 Peter 5:8)*? Know that when you are doing anything in God's name, persecution will come *(2 Timothy 3:12).*

But would it surprise you to know that 99.7% of the harshest criticism and personal mistreatment I've received comes from those who claim Christ?

Not counting conversations where people asked tough questions to genuinely understand more about the ministry. Not including difficult conversations that were intended for my good. I am simply referring to messages I've gotten from people who share that they are also a believer in Christ, then continue to directly attack or question God's calling on my life without the use of any Scripture and without the context of a personal relationship with me.

To break down the math, an average of two or three messages like this come in each week. Over six years, that adds up to just under 1,000 of these types of conversations.

But those same six years, I can only recall ***three*** incidences that involved non-believers.

Three as opposed to over nine hundred. Don't miss the point. This is not about me. And I don't experience near the scrutiny that some of God's warriors are faced with because they have many more eyes on them than I do. But I've talked to several other ministry leaders who have confirmed similar statistics in their own lives. I simply use that number to illustrate a point:

If those in ministry were not consistently tempted to be distracted, derailed or discouraged by our own brothers & sisters in Christ, how much further could the gospel message be?

Think about it. Do you ever wonder why Christianity isn't more of a force in the world? With the power of the one true God and the truth and life of Jesus Christ, why isn't Christianity the fastest growing religion in today's world?

Of course, we know that we have a real enemy who is relentless in pursuing his pointless battle, despite knowing his schemes are already void because of Jesus' death on the cross. Though the war is already won, he remains persistent due to little victories he gets each day when he is able to derail and distract those who are pursuing Christ or to keep others in darkness for another day.

We may not be able to harness Satan's hustle ourselves, but we can certainly refuse to stall any Kingdom progress being made by silencing our critical spirits against other believers.

I'll confess that I haven't done this perfectly myself. One incident I remember in particular: There was a certain preacher I found myself constantly criticizing. I said things about how his teaching was "watered down" and referred to his sermons as "prosperity gospel." Many times, I did this without being prompted by the Holy Spirit. I initiated the criticism on my own.

But then, something happened. A couple I had been praying to come to Christ for five years started attending church regularly. I began seeing the husband share things he was learning from reading the Bible daily. The next time I saw them, his eyes lit up as he began gushing about his pastor and the truths he was learning.

I was elated. Overjoyed. I shed a few tears, thinking of all the prayers God had graciously answered. "So, what made you decide to attend church that first time?" I asked him.

Insert conviction. Turns out, the very pastor I had criticized in the past was who God had used as a gateway to pique the curiosity of this sweet couple. In a raw moment with God, I had to repent of my own critical spirit.

Now, we don't have to condone the actions, beliefs or teachings of everyone who claims Christ, but we also don't need to waste our energy condemning them.

Consider the attitude of the apostle Paul: *"But what does it matter? The important thing is that in every way, whether from false motives or true, Christ is preached. And because of this I rejoice. Yes, and I will continue to rejoice" (Philippians 1:18).*

So publicly, let's teach truth. And publicly, let's rejoice whenever Christ is proclaimed, trusting that His Word never returns void *(Isaiah 55:11)*, and leave motives up for God to determine.

But publicly, we must also think beyond our selfish needs to be "right" or "better" than someone else and think with the person far from Christ in mind. If they see that we can't even get along with one another, why would they ever become interested in linking arms with us?

• ***When we spend our time judging others, we miss fixing what's wrong in our own heart that is separating us from God.*** *"Why do you see the speck that is in your brother's eye, but do not notice the log that is in your own eye? Or how can you say to your brother, 'Let me take the speck out of your eye,' when there is the log in your own eye? You hypocrite, first take the log out of your own eye, and then you will see clearly to take the speck out of your brother's eye."* (Matthew 7:3-5)

Billy Graham once wrote, "It is always difficult and dangerous to attempt to list sins according to their degree of seriousness. In one sense, all sins are equal in that they all separate us from God. The Bible's statement, *"For the wages of sin is death ..."* (Romans 6:23), applies to all sin, whether in thought, word, or deed."

All sin, whether we've made them little or big in our minds, separate us from God and should be dealt with according to that realization. The realization that we have all fallen short of the glory of God. And the more time we let go by where we concentrate more on fixing the sins of others rather than focusing on our own hearts, the further and further we will be separated from Him.

I left this point for last because if we get this one right, the rest will take care of themselves. The next time we feel the need to correct someone else, what if we instead asked:

> *"God, what's wrong in my heart that I need You to correct first?"*

Let's open our mouths in wisdom, and keep them shut the rest of the time.

#P31Prayer

Lord, we confess that we are not short on our opinions. But God, most of the time, our opinion is not needed; Your truth is. Help us to open our mouths with wisdom and to discern when it's best that we keep our mouths shut. But God, we can't open our mouths in wisdom if we don't rely on You. Help us to be disciplined to grow in our knowledge of You daily. But don't let the knowledge just stay in our heart. Instead, let your knowledge change how we live, which, in turn, will be a powerful witness to those around us. God, whenever we are tempted to judge others or to get involved in situations that don't affect us, please help us to retrain our brains to ask You what areas of our lives need Your correction. Help us to be encouragers to all, but God, increase our encouragement for others who are pursuing You. We don't know the exact battle everyone is fighting, but we do know that all believers have a real enemy. Help us to walk as intentional allies, considering others as more significant than ourselves, just as Jesus did. Thank You for His example, and thank You for who You are. We love You. Amen.

#P31Practice

In today's world, we have so many platforms to air our opinions. Platforms don't have to be earned anymore. If you can create a social media account, you can have a platform where you're free to voice your opinion.

And because we have more places to publicly share our opinion, we have even more opportunities to say something that we shouldn't. It increases our need for discernment and wisdom in opening our mouths.

I don't agree with all memes, but I laughed out loud at the one I saw that said, "My opinion was completely changed by your unrequested rant on social media." – Said No One Ever

Here are my two rules that I use to approach sharing on social media:

- ***I won't type anything I wouldn't say to a person's face or into a microphone.***

Most of us are much more brave behind a computer screen. Sometimes, it's not even brave; it's just dumb. It's so easy to either say something we will regret or take something that should remain private and blast it into a public forum.

Apply this quick test, and you may save yourself an argument and/or embarrassment.

- ***Put a greater filter on the question social media asks.***

One of the most popular social media platforms is still Facebook. We log in, and there's that question: *What's on your mind?*

For the love of Pete, will someone please tell Mark Zuckerberg that's a terrible question to ask? Most of the time, no one needs to know what's on our mind!

Here's the question I ask myself before posting: "What can I share that will encourage and benefit whoever reads it?"

For a season, I even created my own post-it note and stuck it on my laptop.

Remember God's instruction: *"Do not let any unwholesome talk come out of your mouths, but only what is helpful to building others up according to their needs, that it may benefit those who listen."* (Ephesians 4:29)

Do you need to re-think how you use social media? There's so much discouragement and negativity in our world. Will you assume the responsibility to be a positive voice of truth and encouragement to a world starved for light?

Let's be better, and let's do it together.

Is there anything I need to correct in how I use social media?

____

____

____

____

____

How can I be a better encouragement on social media?

____

____

____

____

____

day twenty-six

#P31Goal

My words and actions serve as loving instruction for others.

#P31Authority

She opens her mouth in wisdom, and ***the teaching of kindness is on her tongue.*** Proverbs 31:26

#P31Encouragement

For such a tiny muscle, the tongue has a lot of power. In fact, God's Word reminds us *"the tongue has the power of life and death"* (Proverbs 18:21).

But instead of understanding today's phrase to mean teaching others about kindness, though that's certainly part of it, it's much easier to think of this as being focused on "loving instruction."

The word from the original Hebrew was a broader word that spread deeper than her words, letting us know that it's referring to how she lives her life in addition to what she says. Her walk matches her talk. Words and actions both matter.

If our lives don't match what we teach, our words are useless. But our words validate the reason behind our actions.

Perhaps you've heard someone quote before, "Preach the gospel. Use words if necessary." My pastor, Bruce Frank, quipped once, "That's like saying, 'Here's my phone number. If necessary, use numbers.'"

Yes, we are supposed to be living examples of His message, but knowledge of the truth requires our words.

Ed Stetzer put it this way: "The gospel is not habit, but history. The gospel is the declaration of something that actually happened. And since the gospel is the saving work of Jesus, it isn't something we can do, but it is something we must announce. We do live out its implications, but if we are to make the gospel known, we will do so through words."[12]

Words and actions are not separate from one another. When they work together and complement one another, we make sure our credibility stays intact.

Our character question for ourselves is this: *"Do our words and actions give **loving instruction** to those around us?"*

Emphasis on the loving. Emphasis on the instruction. Ephesians 4:15 commands, *"We must speak the truth in love."*

Just like our words and actions cannot be absent from one another, truth and love are required to work together.

In our world today, it's too often that we see these traits isolated from another. All truth. Or all love. Both of which are inferior without the other. The absence of one does not represent the fullness of our Savior.

Tim Keller once pointed out, "Truth without love is imperious self-righteousness. Love without truth is cowardly self-indulgence."[13]

---

12 www.christianitytoday.com/edstetzer/2012/june/preach-gospel-and-since-its-necessary-use-words
13 www.desiringgod.org/articles/speaking-truth-in-love

Let's dig a little deeper into how ignoring one or the other are both rooted in selfishness.

• ***Imperious Self-Righteousness: All Truth***

John Newton referred to this mindset as "cruel arrogance." It's the attitude that cannot tolerate the imperfections and shortcomings of another. It's the slippery slope that often leads to believing everyone else's sins are worse than their own.

Think back to when you were growing up. I know for me, it would have been much easier if my parent's had yelled at me. If they had gotten mad, spewed a bunch of words in a hateful way, I could have yelled right back, stormed off to my room, slammed the door, and begin my next plot of how to rebel against them.

But that wasn't their approach. Choosing to speak the truth in love, they often shared with me why my poor choice of action was going to require discipline. My dad would share that he was disappointed and point out that the reason for my punishment was because they loved me too much to let me behave that way.

That led to no storming off to my room. There was no door slam. Whether it happened immediately or it took me longer to swallow my pride, I would eventually acknowledge that they were right, feel conviction of my wrong, and accept their punishment for my good.

Basically, the "truth in love" approach persuades us to listen, whereas the "all truth" approach inspires rebellion. Let's commit to doing the hard but worthy thing and make sure we're saying the right thing in the right way.

• ***Cowardly Self-Indulgence: All Love***

If we don't love someone enough to tell them the truth, we don't really love them.

I'll be honest with you: The Bible brings up a lot of hard questions, and I can't answer them all other than to say, "He is God, and I am not."

But I do know we were born sinful. Often, our natural inclination is to please ourselves. We don't all struggle with the same sins, but we all have a sin problem, and Jesus is the only solution for it.

And I do believe His Word is clear on which paths lead to sin and destruction and which path leads to light and righteousness.

Why might we struggle with different sins? Maybe it's just like how are gifts and talents weave together to make us stronger together. If one stumbles, there should be a pack of us right there to lovingly pick our sister up and help set her back on the right path.

But it's not loving her if we let her continue to trip over and over again. It's not loving her if we don't uncover her eyes to her blind spot. It's not comfortable. It's messy. It's hard. And, quite honestly, when truth in love is not received, it really hurts.

But it's worth it. Jesus said, "*If you hold to My teaching, you are really my disciples. Then you will know the truth, and the truth will set you free*" (John 8:32).

God's truth does not limit us. It frees us to be all that God has created us to be. That's what we deny someone when we deny them God's truth. Let's refuse to let others be enslaved to sin or deceived by Satan. And we can only do that by or loving them enough to tell them the truth.

Let's show others the depths of our hearts rather than giving them pieces of our minds.

#P31Prayer

God, help us to be "loving instruction" to those around us. God, help our actions to create a curiosity in others to know more about You. But God, don't let us think our actions alone can save. Only Your truth sets us free, and that requires us being bold enough to let our words back up our behavior. God, it's so hard to get this one right. It requires that we abandon our selfishness, whether we're tempted to elevate ourselves and look down upon others' sin in arrogance with an "all truth" approach, or we cowardly refuse to pick up a weaker believer because we might face their rejection. Help us to remember that Your acceptance is the only acceptance that matters. Not loving others to restoration and being all that You have called them to be is too steep a price to pay for our own comfort. Help us to say the right thing in the right way. Help our actions to pave the way for others to listen. May we be humble enough to apologize to others when we don't do this correctly. And when we get it right, Lord, help us to remember that it's not our doing, but You in us, that makes it possible. We love you. Amen.

#P31Practice

Speaking the truth in love is so hard to put into practice. Several years ago, I had the pleasure to listen to Francis Chan speak to a group of leaders, and he offered us seven questions to ask ourselves before we teach God's truth.

I keep these questions at the front of my Bible. Whether I am preparing a message for a group of ladies or preparing for a difficult conversation with another believer, I make myself examine my heart to see if my teaching passes the test of these questions. I pray they are as helpful to you as they are to me.

Questions to ask before I speak:

Am I more concerned with what others/this person will think or what God thinks?

Do I genuinely love these people/this person?

Am I accurately representing God's truth?

Have I applied my words to my own life?

Am I depending on the Holy Spirit's power or my own cleverness?

Will this message/conversation draw attention to me or to God?

Does this audience/person really need this message?

day twenty-seven

#P31Goal

I prioritize intentional living and purposeful focus inside my home.

#P31Authority

She looks well to the ways of her household, *and does not eat the bread of idleness.* Proverbs 31:27

#P31Encouragement

Let's be honest: There's a lot that goes into running a household well. The sheer logistics are enough for a full to-do list, and as we all know, that is only the beginning of the responsibility. With each person that lives in our household, that not only adds one more person's schedule, but another person that needs our time, attention, affection and priority focus.

But here's the problem: We often consider household responsibilities as inevitable. They have to get done, so they'll get done. So rather than careful consideration, household responsibilities frequently get done in our frazzled, last-minute moments, or they don't get done at all.

I've seen it (and experienced it first-hand in my own life) over and over again. Even the most focused and diligent woman in most areas tends to fly by the seat of her pants at home.

Can you relate?

Here's what I know for sure. You would not have picked up this book if it were not your heartbeat that God has first place in your life, and that your family comes second. The fact that the title intrigued you speaks volumes about the desires of your heart.

So if our desire is that God is first and our family is second, why does our calendar often reflect different priorities?

If we were to write down everything we do, from Facebook, Netflix, text messages, and web surfing to work, running errands, cooking and cleaning and, *gasp,* even serving, we'd probably be embarrassed by the small sacrifices of time that we offer to God and the emotional and spiritual well-being of our families.

So while I do think that having systems in place for the logistics of our homes to run smoothly is important, I want to focus today on the lasting impact and opportunity we have for influence that exists inside our homes.

Chew on these words from Andy Stanley: "Your greatest contribution to the Kingdom of God may not be something you do, but someone you raise."

If our priorities are not in the right place, we could miss the chance of our greatest Kingdom contribution.

Priority-Based Living: Faith-first, family-focused

• ***Faith-first:***

"Looking well" to the ways of our household means that we prioritize our time spent with God. I'm often reminded of the story of Mary and Martha *(Luke 10:38-42).* I so desperately want to be a Mary, sitting at the feet of Jesus, soaking up His wisdom, but I know I have more Martha tendencies than I care to admit. I often struggle with getting distracted by small tasks that could easily derail me from the big picture of what it most important.

Even if, like Martha, I am busy with good things.

Martha had Jesus and the disciples in her home. Talk about hostess pressure! She was cooking and serving all alone in the kitchen. Naturally, it didn't take long for her to get frustrated that her sister was just sitting there "doing nothing."

While we may never entertain Jesus in our home, certainly, we can relate to being so busy doing things for Jesus that we're distracted us from Jesus.

He's just as real now as He was then.

This isn't an excuse to not serve. We've already established that serving in areas that God has gifted us puts the talents and abilities He entrusted to us to excellent use. But we can't miss the main thing.

We find time to do what matters to us most. Bottom line. How else would you have binge-watched that entire series on Netflix? Or made hand-made teacher gifts that were totally Pinterest-worthy during one of your busiest weeks?

If we make ourselves too busy to spend time with God, we are robbing ourselves of blessing. The blessing of sitting at His feet. The blessing of His wisdom. The blessing of His comfort and presence.

Imagine your most inconvenient moment. But if someone you respect said, "Let me teach you something that will change you forever," wouldn't you find the time to listen?

That's what time in God's presence does. Reading His Word transforms our minds. Seeking His wisdom positions us exactly where He wants us. Time in prayer softens our hearts for others and deepens our personal relationship with Him.

And it's that consistent, priority slot. Just like infrequent workouts won't produce a rock hard body, infrequent time spent with God won't develop a rock-solid relationship with Christ.

And bottom line: We can't give to others what we don't have ourselves. If we want to be a spiritual influence in our family's lives, we have to be influenced by God first.

As I mentioned earlier, we joke in my household that nobody wants to be around mama until mama has been with Jesus...but it's not really a joke. I need Him daily, speaking His truth over my life. I've attempted living life my way, and I've proven that in myself, I have the ability to be pretty destructive to myself and those around me.

Let's never allow ourselves to be too prideful to remember what our lost lives were like without Him. Let's refuse to be too busy to be blessed in His presence.

- ***Family-focused:***

Distraction is everywhere. More distractions exist today than ever before. I mean, did you ever think you would carry a computer around in your hand? You can schedule your kid's orthodontist appointment, close a business deal, tell a friend happy birthday, and send a letter to your Compassion child in less than 10 minutes, all from your fingertips...literally.

So here's the question I want to ask: What gets the most of our intentionality? Where does the majority of our focus go?

If the answer to that question is not our walk with the Lord and our families, then, friend, we are missing it!

Too often, we allow ourselves to be distracted. In trying to do too many things at once, nothing gets our best. We attempt to have an after-school conversation with our kids while we're trying to send that last-minute email we never got around to, and we miss the catch in their throat when they're answering our questions about how their day was.

We miss their hurt...not because we're not good moms. Not because we don't have good intuition. Simply because we made the choice to allow ourselves to be distracted.

Are we going to pick up on everything? Probably not. I wish I could guarantee us otherwise. But I do know for sure that we will always have the opportunity to pursue motherhood distracted.

Or focused.

Let's put the phone down. Let's turn the TV off. Let's look one another in the eye and not ever give our husbands or our kids a reason to believe that some device is more important to us than them.

Intentional focus. Purposeful living. It's even more important inside our homes than it is outside of them.

#P31Prayer

God, thank you so much for the responsibility of managing a household. Give us the diligence to pursue this responsibility as a priority in our lives. God, we know this doesn't mean we have to do it all ourselves in order to be a godly woman. But we must create the system of how the logistics all take place, so we boldly ask You for wisdom and discernment as we make those decisions. But God, more importantly, help us to realize the ministry opportunities that exist inside our homes. We have so much Kingdom-influence in the relationships You have given us there. Don't let us get distracted, God, even with good things. We don't want to end up so busy with good things that we miss out on the best that You have planned for us. Help us to prioritize time at Your feet. Help us to remember what we're really missing out on when we skip our time with You. We want to crave You, Lord. We know You have placed a void in our lives that only You can fill. We pray that void would overwhelm our souls so much that we come running to Your presence to be filled. And God, just as You are always available to us, help us to put that characteristic on display to our families. We don't want to be distracted or divided with them, Lord. Give us Your insight to help us be spiritually and emotionally in tune with our husbands and children. Provide Your wisdom and comfort for us to pass on to them. Don't let us settle for distracted, unfocused lives. Thank you for leading our path in this way. Help us stick closely to You and not fall for worldly schemes and counterfeit offers. We love you. Amen.

#P31Practice

Today is going to involve some writing. If you love journaling, you are going to love this exercise. But even if you dread journaling, you will be so grateful you completed this application.

When I first completed this exercise, I had no idea the impact it would have on my life. Thankfully, this exercise helped me be ahead of the storm. I created it before I needed it. So if you find yourself thinking you don't need this yet, fantastic! You're setting yourself up for future success. Don't miss this chance.

Write a priority clarity statement.

This is an exercise I was encouraged to do from one of my business mentors, Chalene Johnson[14]. Chalene is the creator behind many fitness programs, but most recently, has transitioned into an online business mentor, creating programs such as Smart Success and the Marketing Impact Academy. I got her permission to share this tidbit with you from *Smart Success:* writing a priority clarity statement.

This brings extreme clarity in decision-making. Often, the most important decisions are not made in the moment, but are prayerfully decided before the problem is present. For example, I'm grateful before I even went on my first date, my parents and godly influences in my life encouraged me to make the decision to wait to be sexually intimate until I was married. I'm extremely grateful that I didn't have to attempt to figure out what my convictions were in the midst of a weak moment.

When you write a priority clarity statement, you must clearly articulate three things:

1) Name the priority.
2) Identify the steps you will take to put action to your words.
3) Determine the results that will clearly mark that this priority has root in your life.

---

[13] www.chalenejohnson.com - *I highly recommend her Smart Success Academy that she opens once a year.*

Just one month after I wrote my statement for the first time, I was faced with a decision. A travel opportunity presented itself with my job. In addition to having one child still nursing under the age of one, I had a prior volunteer speaking engagement I was committed to at a church. My husband also had commitments with his job at our church that same weekend.

Even with getting my parents involved, the logistics were quickly evolving into a nightmare. The trip was cross-country, and there was really no way I would be able to make the trip without Cole, who was my youngest at the time. I would need to have a travel companion with me to help with him while I was in meetings, in addition to arranging childcare for my oldest while my husband was busy with ministry commitments that weekend.

Here was the catch: There were significant finances attached to making the trip. Just for showing up, I was guaranteed to add what would be about a 15% bonus to my current annual salary.

Feeling frustrated, frazzled and stressed, I pulled out my priority clarity statement. One quick read of my statement, and I felt immediate peace: I didn't need to make the trip.

So I didn't. My priority clarity statement clearly identifies God and my family over any career or financial gain. Suddenly, that "hard choice" wasn't even a decision anymore. It was just a phone call, where I politely declined the opportunity.

Years later, I still have peace about that decision because it honors my priorities. If I had made a different choice, I have no doubt that I would have regrets.

Here's mine as a sample to get your wheels turning:

> *The spiritual and emotional well-being of my family is my top priority, which I honor by staying personally grounded in prayer and God's Word daily, as well as being mentally and physically present and actively involved in the lives of my husband and children. I will never allow a financial or career opportunity to cause my family or faith to take a back seat. I will truly treasure these years while my children are at home*

with me by being an engaging, loving, playful and intentional mom. I will prioritize work-related calls/ meeting/conference calls/appearances when they are napping, in bed for the night on a few nights a week that James and I decide together, or fully engaged in the care of someone else for a small percentage of hours each week. I will know I am honoring this priority when it is clear to everyone who knows me that my faith and my family are more important to me than any personal or financial pursuit.

I will strive to improve my marriage by praying for James specifically based on his current needs daily, as well as being loving, romantic, respectful and supportive of where God has currently called him. I will know I am being a role model of a godly wife when we are laughing consistently and completely at peace with our God-given roles from Ephesians 5:22-33.

I will work to teach our children to love God first, others second, and themselves last. I will know I am honoring this priority when I see them living out Luke 2:52 – growing in wisdom, stature, and in favor with God and man.

I will honor the spiritual well-being of my family by producing fruit with my life, practicing the spiritual disciplines of reading God's Word, prayer, service, generosity and using my God-given abilities faithfully, pointing all glory back to Him. I will pray and read the Bible with our kids at bedtime, naptime, or both. We will serve together as a family, both on our own as God leads, and as active members of the body of Christ, partnering with the local church. I will know I am honoring this priority when our children accept Christ at a young age and they marry godly spouses.

I honor the emotional well-being of my family by making each of them feel valued and central to my personal happiness. In addition to "unplugging" one full weekend day, I will also commit to leaving my cell phone on the charger/airplane mode during all mealtimes with family. I will know I am honoring this priority when my husband and children do not resent my job/phone/computer.

I will decline any opportunity that might place demands on my schedule from an outside force. I will diligently seek to use my calling/passion, but in a way that allows me to work from home. I will think big/global by using the Internet to utilize my gifts, as opposed to traveling extensively. I will decline any opportunity that might place stress, unnecessary demands on my family, or prevent us from being able to worship together on Sundays.

James and I will work together so our children know that after Jesus, they are the most important people in our lives. We will make our commitment to our family known publically, especially when it comes to our careers. James and I will commit to at least one date night out per month, while prioritizing weekly date nights in. I will prioritize weekly focused playtime with my kids and squeeze in one-on-one time with each of them regularly. We will sacrifice and do whatever steps are necessary to send them to a school that honors the Lord. We will know we are honoring this priority when our children never doubt the love James and I have for God, for one another or for them.

My Priority Clarity Statement:

day twenty-eight

#P31Goal

I keep my heart and mind in gear with God's purposes.

#P31Authority

She looks well to the ways of her household, and ***does not eat the bread of idleness.*** Proverbs 31:27

#P31Encouragement

If you've made it this far in our study together, I'm going to assume that idleness is not a part of your vocabulary. In fact, you have so much going on in your life, I'm going to imagine you view laziness more as a luxury than a hindrance in your life.

Because I know the woman I have with me here, I don't want

to waste my breath telling you to become an active participant of your life and not avoid doing work. You get that. We've fully established that, in order to accurately represent the P31 woman, we must live purposeful lives.

But there are two sides of idleness I want to address that I pray will minister to you as much as God has convicted me to change in my own life.

• ***Rest Vs. Idle***

Rest is not the same thing as being idle. As Aedriel Moxley put it so eloquently, "Lord, help me not confuse rest with being unproductive."

Confession: I totally stink at resting. I'm two for two so far on kids who are early risers and not-so-great at napping. My husband is often quick to point out they inherited those traits from me.

My kids have helped me slow down a lot. I am much more likely to be content in my pajamas on the couch if I have one of them curled up beside me. But it's not in my nature to prioritize rest.

But God did. On the seventh day, He rested (*Genesis 2:2*).

God certainly didn't rest because He had to. I believe He rested to set an example for us and to take the time to truly enjoy His creation. P.S. I'm totally guilty of that, too. I tend to move on too quickly from project to project, without giving proper praise to God for the work He has done.

It may seem like a silly question to ask, but I'm going to do it anyway: Do you rest in Him enough? Or do you inaccurately view "rest" as a waste of your time?

To my sister who struggles taking a day off, I can relate. But in His Word, God clearly asks us to reserve one day where our energy and focus is reserved for Him, not ourselves:

> *Remember the Sabbath day by keeping it holy. Six days you shall labor and do all your work, but the seventh day is a Sabbath to the Lord your God.*
> Exodus 20:8-10a

Again, I want you to think of this as a matter of heart, not logistics. Here's the question:

> ***Do you take one day a week that is more focused on Him than on you?***

On paper, that's easy to answer. Of course, we would say yes. But what do our actions say?

If our actions continue to work, continue to strive, continue to grind, without time for proper rest and for Him to pour back into us, we're not "refusing to quit." We're stubbornly refusing to submit to living His way.

Rest is not idle. Rest is not purposeless. Rest is following in the example that we were given and slowing down enough to allow God to speak, restore and rejuvenate us for what we have ahead.

Rest also doesn't mean that we aren't allowed to minister to others. In fact, you may find that on the days you maintain the slowest pace, you have the greatest opportunity to do ministry.

But we must remember that ministry overflows from His strength in us, not our own supply. Therefore, if we are truly abiding in Him, we will never be too exhausted to do God's work.

Oswald Chambers may have said it best: "It is impossible to get exhausted in work for God. We get exhausted because we try to do God's work in our own way."

Let's refuse to rob ourselves of the blessing available to us that comes with living God's way. Our striving and driving may result in good things. But when we refuse to submit the smallest area of our lives over to total obedience to God, we place a limitation on ourselves.

I'm reminded of words of my friend, Jess Connolly: "In my own strength, I may do many good things. But there will be no power."

Do you want to be limited to the blessing and good things that you can do in your own strength? Or do you want full access to His power?

Let's go back to the reference I gave from Exodus 20 earlier. Too often, we think of this verse as telling us what we can't do, but we refuse to focus on what it tells us to do: Keep that day holy.

If we're honest, this command is like a "time tithe." God asks for 10% of our resources, but with this command, He's asking us for 1/7 of our time.

Another heart check question: Do we trust Him with 1/7 of our productivity?

In our hearts, we know He's good for it. Don't we know God can do more in six days than we could ever accomplish in seven?

This is another act of faith and obedience. It's another way to show that our trust is more in Him than in ourselves. It's not a spiritually intelligent decision to put more stock in ourselves or in the things of this world than in God.

We have to go against normal logic. Logic tells us that the more time we spend working and grinding, the more results we will get. But our heart knowledge of wisdom that comes from God lets us know otherwise. Doing things His way always reaps the best results.

God doesn't tell us to rest in order to set us back, sister. He tells us to rest so that He can set us up to do more with Him than we could ever do ourselves.

• ***Deep Over Wide***

If we aren't careful, we can fall victim to the masses-mentality. It's too easy to think that, even in ministry, the masses are all that matter.

> *"I'd do things with more excellence if there were more people involved."*
>
> *"As soon as we get more people plugged in, I'll devote more time and energy."*

First of all, that's completely backwards to logic. The more your responsibility increases, the more issues you will have that divide your time. More people will never create more time for you to do a better job.

It's also not how God works. He tells us that when we are faithful with little, we can be trusted with much *(Luke 16:10)*. Not "do average work with a little, and I'll see if it's just because you didn't have enough responsibility."

Is that not enough? The masses-mentality is also not how Jesus lived. Jesus spoke to crowds, yes. But He always made time for the one. He didn't put less energy, effort or focus on those moments.

Think about Zaccheus *(Luke 19, if you need to refresh your memory)*. There was a huge crowd in Jericho that had gathered to see Jesus. Being small, Zaccheus couldn't see over the crowd, so he climbed up in a tree, just to get a glimpse of Jesus walking by.

As he passed the tree, Jesus looked up and said, "Zaccheus, come down, for today, I must stay at your house."

Jesus drowned out the crowd to see the one.

Zaccheus turned from his sinful ways, gave half of his possessions to the poor, and paid back the money he had stolen from others times four. He confessed faith in Jesus, and he was saved.

But let me blow your mind a little more. I heard this story countless times as a kid, and I never understood this part until I was an adult. Jesus was coming through Jericho on his journey to Jerusalem. *His last trip to Jerusalem.*

That's right. Jesus was intentional to reach Zaccheus on the road to be crucified.

So whether you feel like you're a leader in ministry or not, if you're a Christian, we have been given the same responsibility. As Christians, we would do a much better job of getting the message of Jesus out if we took our one-by-one opportunities as seriously as we hope those preaching to the multitudes take handling the gospel.

By the way, there's no finger-pointing involved in this, except for the one pointing at me. I know I can get sucked into the world of likes, double taps, hearts, crowds, and masses as much as anyone. *(More on that tomorrow!)*

My sweet friend, Kelly Wendorff, summed it up this way: "Souls over goals."

Let's not forget that in living like Jesus, Jesus came for all, but

He also came for the one. *"For the Son of Man has come to seek and to save that which was lost"* (Luke 19:10).

Souls over goals, friends. The one is just as important as the crowd. Eternity matters for all, yes, but it does not matter less for the one.

Not once in God's Word does He attach an assignment that He gives with a number. He always lays the mission on the heart of His servant, but God doesn't assign a number. That's worldly pressure that we've put on ourselves to impress others.

Here's what we know: Depth is our job. How deep will we love? How deep will we serve? That's what He calls us to.

Then, God determines the width. He gives the growth. As Paul acknowledged to the church at Corinth, *"I planted, Apollos watered, but God gave the growth"* (1 Corinthians 3:6).

Let's make sure our hearts don't get idle because the masses aren't there. Let's make sure our hearts and minds are aligned with His. St. Augustine so accurately captured the heart of God when he said, "God loves each of us as if there were only one of us."

Let's give our all for the one today. And every day after.

#P31Prayer

God, help us to give You glory with the way we spend our time. This may mean working at a different pace than the world does. We might get momentarily lapped on this earth. But God, we're not running the rat race of the world. We are running Your race. We are running toward Your finish line. God, we know that the call and the assignment that You have for each of us will not look exactly like someone else's assignment. So the only way to make sure we have our correct orders from You is to make sure we are taking that productive time to step back from the world and find rest in You. God, absolutely protect our hearts against laziness. Fill us with an unquenchable desire to make You famous. May the work that You have called us to do invite people to know You and to give You glory. Give us peace with where You have called us, and help us to serve well where we are. But God, don't let us get it twisted and believe that we are able to do anything that is best outside of Your power. Help us to submit to Your way. Help us to trust you with 1/7 of our time and productivity. God, we know You're good for it. Help our hearts and minds to stay aligned with yours. Help us to define success Your way, not the world's way. Help us to be faithful with our little so our actions show You that we can be trusted with more. We trust Your timing and Your way. We love You. Amen.

#P31Practice

Yesterday, we wrote a priority clarity statement. Today, I want you to define what "success" means for you. In the business world, success is a word we cannot avoid. But we can make sure we have our own definition of what success means to us so we don't get derailed by someone else's definition.

For example, some may define success as prosperity: money, career advancement, a bigger house/better car. Others may define success as more freedom to spend more time with the people they love.

So here's what we need to realize: Success is extremely personal. Success is achieving one's own goals. In fact, one of the quickest ways not to succeed is to succeed at someone else's definition of success.

How do you define success? Write down your definition, and put it somewhere you will see it regularly. Then, live by it.

Here's mine:

> ***Success is obedience to God.***

Attempting to live up to the world's standard of success will leave us exhausted and empty. But living obedient lives to God replaces worldly pressure and feelings of inadequacy with the truth that His way is always the best way, because His purposes prevail. Cheap success is shallow. It ends with me. But real success elevates my God, not me. I don't want people to want my life. I want them to want my Source of life.

I'll share a few of my favorite quotes with you to get your wheels turning as you write your definition of success:

> *"Success is not what you have done compared to what others have done. Success is what you have done compared to what you were created to do."* Tony Evans

> *"Our greatest fear should not be of failure, but of succeeding at things in life that don't really matter."* Francis Chan

> *"God's work done in God's way will never lack God's supplies."* Hudson Taylor

> *"He who lays up treasures on earth spends his life backing away from his treasures. To him, death is loss. He who lays up treasures in heaven looks forward to eternity; he's moving daily toward his treasures. To him, death is gain."* Randy Alcorn

> *God does not give us everything we want, but He does fulfill His promises, leading us along the best and straightest paths to Himself."* Dietrich Bonhoeffer

> *"Our willingness to make others a success is a great measure of the purity of our ambitions."* Dave Harvey

> *"Success is when the people who know you best respect you most."* Mark Batterson

My Definition of Success:

day twenty-nine

#P31Goal

My highest praise comes from those who are closest to me.

#P31Authority

*Her **children rise up and bless her; her husband also and he praises her,** saying, 'Many daughters have done nobly, but **you excel them all.*** Proverbs 31:28-29

#P31Encouragement

I call it the "Proverbs 31:28" test, and I ask myself this question every night before I fall asleep:

From the way I lived my life today, would

my highest praise come from my husband and children?

Anybody can impress someone from afar. Social media makes it pretty easy to post a highlight reel of our lives. With the right filters and edits, we can make our lives appear pretty perfect.

But we can't filter and fool those who see us day-in and day-out. So even if you are not married yet, the implication of this verse for our character is the same; this is an authenticity check:

Are we the real deal, or are we attempting to fake it 'til we make it?

Let's chat about social media for a second. If I asked you to guess how many Facebook posts you "liked," or how many Instagram photos earned your double tap yesterday, what number would you say? Think about it.

Got your number? Okay. Now, a harder question. No matter what number you listed, could you tell me any specifics from just three of the posts that earned your approval yesterday?

If you're like the majority I've polled in person, you can't. The average number others gave me was 100, and they couldn't articulate three of the posts.

So if we know that to be true of ourselves and others, *why do we allow ourselves to be so approval-addicted to what people think of us online?*

You know what I'm talking about. That incessant, nagging "refresh" sweep of your thumb after you've posted. Whether it's business related or we just "need" others to affirm how cute our kids are, why do we allow ourselves to care so much that we are willing to plant our faces in our phones and refresh every few seconds to see if anyone else has affirmed us?

Because we are seeking approval from the wrong sources. It's easy to click the "Like" button or the double tap. It's much more difficult to earn verbal praise from those who see us at our worst.

But if it's their praise that means the most to us, we must be willing to do the work necessary to earn it.

So, it was hard to articulate the social media posts you approved in the last 24 hours. But what about the kindest things your husband and children have said to you ever? Even if it was a compliment you received from your husband years ago, can you remember every single detail, from his words to what you were wearing when he said it?

I know I can. Because my family's words have weight in my life.

My kids are still young, but I pray I'll never forget what it sounded like when my 5-year old asked me, "Mommy, is Baby Shea going to be as beautiful as you are?" As he looked into my non-make-up face and ran his hands through my hair that had no less than two entire bottles of dry shampoo, I squeezed him tight and said, "At least in your eyes, buddy, I hope not."

There's no amount of social media approval that could ever come close to topping that.

Here's the thing: My family is not perfect. My husband is an amazing man, I love him dearly, and we are always willing to fight for our marriage, but life is never boring when two opinionated people live under the same roof. And while that's the sweetest story ever about my Noah above, I could also tell you about the time he wanted to hide his brother in the dryer. Or the time his brother drew on hardwood floor with a Sharpie. You get the picture.

But even in the midst of their craziness and my husband's countless attempts to ruin all the fun in everything with his endless efforts to condense our lives into a spreadsheet *(still love you, Boo)*, our messy, imperfect lives are the best part of my day. Every. Single. Day.

Here's the truth: If the best part of our day happens on social media, we've missed it.

I'm not going to pretend like I dislike social media, because I don't. It's a fantastic tool, and I believe when used properly, God can get glory from it. But it's a tool that can too easily become a trap if we don't set appropriate parameters.

A trap that leads to meaningless approval-addiction, comparison, and perhaps the most covert trap – missing what's happening right in front of us. We must be cautious not to miss the greatest opportunities for influence that God has given us – the ones that happen in the moment right where we are.

When we do that, we earn praise from those who are closest to us, spend the most time with us, live with us, and see us at our worst...because they know that the woman we are on social media is the same woman we are at home. In fact, it should be our goal for them to be consistently grateful they get "the real thing."

It's not my goal to belittle your potential for influence and impact outside of your home. But we must examine our hearts.

Since we already know that being wife to our husbands and mom to our children are assignments God has given only to us and we never have to question those callings, the best indicators of our value and worth exists inside our hearts and our homes. God's approval and praise from our husband and children should be the bulk of our approval list.

If there's one piece of advice I find myself giving over and over again, it's this: ***Shorten your approval list.*** Please tuck in deep your heart and apply it. There is so much freedom that exists when that list shrinks.

We are called to be people-lovers, not people-pleasers. There's a distinct difference between the two. And the truth is, when we live in radical obedience to God, seeking His approval only, we are able to love others better simply because we are walking closer with God.

If you're His, He has already stamped His approval on you. He has placed close relationships around you to provide accountability to walk with Him. And that is more than enough for us.

• ***Praise from Children***

I always feel inadequate addressing parenting issues. After all, I've only been a mom for five years, and I, in no shape or form, have it all figured out. But these are the things I've seen that have helped me shape a positive relationship with my kids, as well as lessons I've learned from my mentors.

• ***Pursue pure hearts, not just good behavior.***
The truth is, our heart is on display with our behavior. But behavior can also be manipulated; the heart cannot. For example, have you ever heard your child say, "I'm sorry" to their sibling, even though their tone and glare that accompanied their words indicated they were only sorry they got caught, or maybe sorry that mom and dad were watching? From a young age, we can help them understand that doing the right thing with the wrong motives is still wrong.

If we consistently come back to the condition of their heart before God, not just their behavior, we address the root issue, not the temporary malfunction. And even though it may take some time and some children may be more difficult than others, children thrive with structure and consistency.

And bottom line: We cannot fail if we consistently bring their mind back to God. This one truth alone helps them understand God in the context of a relationship, not rules.

> *Train up a child in the way he should go; even when he is old he will not depart from it.* Proverbs 22:6

• ***Make decisions rooted in what is best for them long-term.***
It's so tempting to do what it easy. To let it go. To appease them in the moment, whether for appearance sake, or just a temporary moment of peace and quiet. But parenting doesn't offer the luxury of the short-term. We are in this for the long-haul, and if we want what's best for them, we must prioritize what shapes their soul, not their moment.

I had a mentor lovingly remind me, "There are no do-overs in motherhood. Make it count."

• ***Say "no" out of necessity, not out of selfishness.***
At the ages of five and two, there are few activities my sons want to do that don't involve a mess. If I base our day around what I want to say "no," to, we would almost never do what they request.

So when they ask to go down to the creek and look for salamanders, or when they ask to get the watercolors out, paint each other with shaving cream or have a water balloon fight, I check my spirit first, and if I have to say "no," I make sure it's because there's a good reason not to, not just because that's not my preference.

But this is about more than pursuing selflessness in parenting. There is something greater at stake.

In the *Mission of Motherhood*, Sally Clarkson put it this way: "Make a list of some things your children like you to do with them but aren't necessarily fun for you... Commit to saying yes to their requests instead of no, *knowing that if you invest in what is important to them, they will be open to believing in what is important to you.*"

• ***Choose joy.***

Let's be real: Sin is often enticing because it looks like it's the most fun option. We have the opportunity to make our homes a fun, welcoming environment. If we're intentional, it can be our children's favorite place to escape, not where they're trying to escape from.

No matter how young our kids are, they understand joy and fun. Despite circumstances, joy is a choice. Let's work to make our homes a joyful place to be.

• ***Aim to be a "because of" parent.***

The opposite is an "in spite of" parent. One day, our kids will either say, "Because of my parents' love...Because of my parents' sacrifice...because of my parents' instruction...because of my parents' example, I choose Jesus."

Or "in spite of." Or worse...they choose differently.

We cannot choose salvation for our children. Ultimately, that personal relationship is between them and God. But we can pursue everything in our power to be "because of" parents.

• ***Praise from Husband***

We've already covered how important it is for us to put in the effort to ensure our husbands get our best, not our leftovers. So without expanding into detail, here are five quick reminders we've already gone over together:

> ***Seek ways to be his helper.***
>
> ***Respect him unconditionally.***
>
> ***Reserve your affection and attention for him.***
>
> ***Give him your best, not your leftovers.***
>
> ***Pray for him and with him.***

But what if I do all of these things, and it doesn't result in praise? What if I've got a prodigal child, or my husband checked out of our marriage years ago?

Be the initiator of praise in your home anyway.

I doubt many relationships have been restored by stonewalling. Refusing to give praise because we know that it's likely not going to be reciprocated will create more tension.

Lay down your pride. Consider others as more important than yourselves. Be the encouraging voice in your home that you wish you heard.

That has way more power to change than adding to the problem.

Quick review:

> *God's approval comes first.*
>
> *Our authenticity is validated when we receive praise from those who know us best.*
>
> *A short list with deep roots defines our real approval better than a long list with a birds-eye view.*
>
> *Earning praise in our homes requires hard, intentional effort.*

We have the ability to initiate praise in our homes, even if it's not reciprocated.

#P31Prayer

God, help us to first seek our worth, callings and approval in You. Help us to be authentic women that prioritize approval in the right places. Don't let us fall into the trap of people-pleasing, but God, help us do the hard work of people-loving. Help our families to get our best, not our leftovers. Help us to tirelessly pursue Your heart and their hearts, and trust You with the rest. God, don't let us settle for the cheap validation that comes from social media and those who only see a glimpse of who we really are. Give us Your eternal perspective to pursue what is true and what is lasting, not what it fake and fleeting. Help us to serve our families selflessly, willingly and with our priority effort. We pray that because of our example, Lord, that our families would walk closer with You. And God, even if we do everything right and we still don't hear audible words of praise from our families, Lord, help Your approval to be enough in our hearts. Send us extra encouragement from You. Remind us that You see everything, Lord, and that nothing done out of obedience is done in vain. Remind us that Your reward and Your forever praise trumps anything this world could offer, even if this world's option seems more appealing. Help us to rest in the truth that Your blessing and reward are always better. We love You. Amen.

#P31Practice

Will you take the social media pledge below to make sure it remains a tool in your life and not a trap? By following this checklist, we ensure that social media adds to our influence and intentionality of life rather than distracting us from what matters most.

Social Media Pledge:

I will:

Reference God's Word more than my phone.

Intentionally allow Jesus to always go before me.

Spend more time in Scripture than scrolling.

Pray more than I post.

Use re-charging my phone as a reminder to re-charge my soul.

Find more satisfaction in obedience to God than applause from others.

Check-in with God each day before I check-in with the world.

(On the next page, re-write the above pledge as your commitment.)

My Social Media Pledge:

day thirty

#P31Goal

Fear of the Lord attains the only lasting praise.

#P31Authority

Charm is deceitful** and **beauty is fleeting, but a woman who fears the Lord, she shall be praised. Proverbs 30:31

#P31Encouragement

I grew up watching *Leave It To Beaver*...in syndication, of course. But when I hear the word "charm," I immediately think of Eddie Haskell.

In case you've never seen the show, Eddie was the sneaky friend of big brother, Wally. He was consistently scheming, coming up with ways for them to get in trouble, always leaving someone else to blame in case they got caught (which they pretty much always did.)

As devious as he was when no adults were around, he was every bit as sickeningly charming when they were present. In a completely over the top way. I mean, what kind of pre-teen boy compliments the outfit or hairstyle of his friend's mother?

But that's the thing about charm: It's not real. It can be taught. It can be turned on and off. It can either be present or non-existent depending on who is in the room.

This verse hits that truth out of the park; it's deceptive. Who wants to build their character on something that is fake?

What about beauty? There's nothing wrong with being beautiful. In fact, there are many godly women in the Bible, such as Esther, that are described as outwardly beautiful. But if that's all we've got, we're in trouble.

Beauty fades. It does not last forever.

Check out this staggering statistic: "If you are under 5'8", above a size 4 dress, or over the age of 20, your chances of getting signed by a major market high fashion/runway agency is about as likely as winning the lottery and getting attacked by a gang of ninjas in the same 24-hour period."[14]

Fantastic. In the beauty industry, if you're 21, you're already washed up.

Beauty is fine, but it's undeserving of our excessive attention because its time for impact on our life is so incredibly short. Don't let it consume your mind.

You are not defined by something as silly as a scale, a mirror, a number, your hair color, your skin tone, your successes or even your failures.

Charm and beauty are human traits that do not last. They might earn us momentary earthly glory, but they won't keep us in the spotlight -- God's or the world's.

Just think about Jesus' triumphant entry in Mark 11. Jesus

---

14 www.modelmayhem.com/education/modeling/2055-how-height-weight-and-age-influence-getting-signed-by-an-agency

entered into Jerusalem, with the people shouting, "Hosanna!" It didn't stop with their exclamation of praise. They also laid their cloaks down and put palm branches down in His path. They recognized Him as God's Son, as the promised One from the line of David.

No doubt, this was a moment of earthly glory. A glamorous moment in the life of Jesus. I mean, it was pretty much modern-day red carpet. Had this happened in 2016, everyone would have been snapping photos, begging for selfies, just aiming to get a glimpse of Jesus so they could tell their friends, "I was there! I saw him!"

That was Sunday.

Tuesday, the plot to kill Jesus began *(Mark 14:1-2)*.

By Thursday evening, He was publicly betrayed by one of His twelve, most trusted followers. He was arrested. He was put on multiple trials, shuffled between the high priest, the Sanhedrin, Herod and Pilate.

He was scourged and beaten. One of his inner circle, Peter, denied Him three times. The people rioted for His crucifixion, even released one of the day's most dangerous criminals for the exchange of Jesus' death. He was mocked with a crown of thorns, forced to carry His own cross, and had nails driven in his hands and feet while the people cheered.

Not to mention, with the exception of John, His mother, and a few other women, Jesus was abandoned by the remaining 10 disciples, who were afraid they themselves would be put to death if they hung around.

And Jesus died a criminal's death on the cross.

Talk about a turnaround.

On Sunday, Jesus is the center of the "red carpet." Five days later, they're delighting at the sight of His red blood.

Five. Days. Later.

Let's not miss the important lesson for us: Earthly glory from charm or beauty may be glamorous, but it is also temporary. *Fleeting. Fickle. Unreliable.*

Simply put, earthly glory without eternal purpose is completely worthless.

Jesus knew the difference. His purpose wasn't persuaded by the glamour of the crowd. Jesus did get His real glory, but it was the result of *being obedient to the point of death.* And it was nothing this world could offer Him.

We see that the same sentiment exists inside the P31 woman: *"But a woman who fears the Lord, she shall be praised."*

Just like Jesus, our lasting glory is wrapped up in our obedience to God.

Being a woman of God's standard has much different requirements than being a woman of the world. Charm and beauty have no bearing on our worth in Him. It's based on obedience. Basically, the way we live our lives shows that what He wants us to do matters more than what we want to do.

Obedience is really not as daunting as we make it out to be. Obedience to God is really only overwhelming if we've entered ourselves into a power struggle with Him.

If we own our main responsibility of living in obedience to Him, there's way more freedom available to us than restriction. Stepping outside of obedience means we've stepped into our feeble attempt to do His job, which is a failed mission before it starts every single time.

Lysa Terkeurst put it simply: "My job is to be obedient to God. His job is everything else."

What we do for Christ is our legacy and what lasts. When this life is over, that's all that will matter. That's what deserves our time and energy, Everything else we invest our time in apart from Him has an expiration date.

Sometimes, we can allow ourselves to get intimidated when we use words like "legacy." We think that means God expects us to do something really big and really significant.

But here's the truth: God can do amazing work with the simplest act of obedience. No obedience is too small or insignificant for Him to use because obedience always takes us one step closer to Him.

As my friend, Pete Wilson, once said: "Life is not about doing great things; it's about doing God things."

Let's not settle for worldly great when godly good is always an option. Let's commit to doing fewer great things and more God things.

"...She shall be praised."

There is praise for doing things God's way, but we can't expect it to be wrapped up in a worldly package. Praise for doing thing God's way comes first from God. We must be spending time with Him to get that affirmation and confirmation from Him.

He is there, sister. He is always reliable. He is the only Constant that exists in our lives. H's our only sure thing. *If we aren't feeling close to Him, God is not the one who stopped speaking.* We must make sure that we are positioned to hear from Him.

Let's finish that story of Jesus. Death had no sting. Jesus rose victoriously on the third day and ascended into heaven to enter His eternal glory, promising His return for those who would remain committed to Him. He gave us His final charge; we are to tell others about Him so as many people as possible can escape the death He died in our place and have eternal life in Heaven.

Following the example of Jesus, let's not fall victim to the fleeting glamorous feeling of the crowd's approval or worldly attributes of charm and beauty. Honor given to us by God is the only approval that exists that is coupled with authority. Therefore, His glory is the only one we should seek.

Jesus' story didn't end on a cross, and if we consume ourselves with living for God's glory, our story won't end in defeat either. Our story will simply be a reflection of His victory.

#P31Prayer

God, help us to focus on the unseen and to build our legacy on what is eternal. Help us to take the time to sit at Your feet and be still before You. Help us seek to please You in obedience above everything else. Make us unaffected by distractions from this world, even if they hold temporary glory for us. We know that Your approval is the only approval that has authority. Fix our eyes solely on You. Help us to be relentless in our pursuit of obedience to You, resting in the truth that Your job is to be concerned with everything else. As we seek to do Your will, give us Your perspective. Give us confirmation as we walk where You have called us. Rather than working for our own fame, name or glory, God, may everything we do be for You. Be our encouragement. Be our validation. Be our approval. Be our worth. Make us women of legacy, not because we do great things, but because we choose to do God things. Thank you for the example of Jesus and for how much You love us. We praise You for His victory and for the path You have marked for us that leads us straight back to You. We love You. Amen.

#P31Practice

"There is not a single Kingdom effort that can happen without some simple, meaningless task." – Curtis Jones

Here's the truth: From the example we see in Jesus and consistent throughout God's Word, God's servants have more moments of grind than glory.

If we're honest, the glory is what we desire. We want that glimpse of God. We want to experience that nearness, closeness and intimacy with Him. Those moments are real, and they're amazing. But we must realize that we must endure a great deal of grind to position ourselves to catch a glimpse of His glory.

Grind examples: Early wake-up calls to spend time with Him, the unique assignments God gives us that the world doesn't understand, and prioritizing serving and worshipping with other believers on Sunday mornings, despite baby sleep schedule disruption, toddler-tantrum wrangling and needing a bulldozer to get your teenager out of bed.

The grind is necessary to get those glory moments. So if we truly want to look different from the world, we will pursue the grind, not the glory.

I'm not sure if it's just the world we live in, but we seem to have even glamourized public ministry. From growing up a worship pastor's kid to being a pastor's wife and serving in public ministry myself, let's set the record straight.

Ministry is not glamorous. It's hard. The glory moments when God shows up makes every grind, every hardship, and every trial worth it. But it's not all spotlights and microphones.

So if the world wants to glamourize every platform, how do we ensure He's getting the glory, not us?

It all goes back to the heart.

Let's journal quick answers to these questions today and spend some extra time in prayer for God to align our hearts with His.

Is there anything in my character that's charming? Something that can be turned on and off or is easily altered depending on the audience?

____

____

____

____

____

____

____

How much time and attention do I spend dwelling on beauty and fleeting attributes of the world?

____

____

____

____

____

____

What does my personal pattern of obedience say about my heart's devotion to Christ?

____

____

____

____

____

____

How do I position myself to get confirmation from God on my life's direction?

What grind will I pursue to ensure that He gets the glory from my life?

day thirty-one

#P31Goal

I humbly serve others to be a blessing, not to be blessed.

#P31Authority

Give her the product of her hands, and let her works praise her in the gates. Proverbs 31:31

#P31Encouragement

If we had to sum up everything we've studied over the last 31 days, here it is: *She selflessly serves to produce results that bring more glory to God than herself and that benefit others more than herself.*

She doesn't neglect herself, but it's not about her. She is successful, but success isn't her motivation. She has thriving relationships with her family, but she tirelessly gives of herself to make them her priority.

I love that the P31 package ultimately boils down to the character trait we've mentioned several times already. A character trait that is an ongoing process that requires a lifetime of effort. And, it's an attribute that completely disappears if we ever feel like we've mastered it...

Humility.

And if we miss humility, we miss it all. As Angela of Foligno said, "Without humility of heart, all the other virtues by which one runs toward God seem – and are – absolutely worthless."

Humility will either be the final touch of our credibility, or our pride will destroy any good we attempt to do.

Our humility is what sets us apart. Because while the woman has a work ethic that cannot be reckoned with, she's not working to benefit herself. She's not working to get some earthly reward.

Her life is about being a blessing, not being blessed.

This is incredibly backward from what we typically see. Most people who work hard do it for the exotic vacations, the huge house, the sweetest ride, the fancy clothes and the luxurious life.

Now, if you have any of the things I mentioned above, that doesn't mean you're not a P31 woman. But if any of those things are our main motivators or our most prized possessions, our intentions might not be as pure as we want to believe.

Let's be honest: we live in a self-promoting world. Working as a business mentor over the last eight years, I've seen far more people who want to be successful than are actually willing to do the work.

But even fewer exist who are willing to do the work to bless someone else more than themselves. Yet, doing just that is what sets us up for a blessing that this world can't even offer.

Here's what we know about our God: With Him, blessing is always forward moving. Consider the words God gave to

Abraham, *"I will bless you... and you will be a blessing" (Genesis 12:2).*

Living our lives to bless others sets us up to be blessed by God. To make sure we understand just how much God is willing to give those who give, let's consider these words of Jesus:

> *Give, and it will be given to you. A good measure, pressed down, shaken together and running over, will be poured into your lap. For with the measure you use, it will be measured to you.* Luke 6:38

Let's take a moment to truly digest the powerful imagery here:

> *"A good measure"*... abundant supply.
>
> *"Pressed down"*... condensed to make room for even more to fit.
>
> *"Shaken together"*... so the contents will combine to take up as little space as possible, again to make room for more.
>
> *"Running over"*... not just filled, but overflowing.
>
> *"Will be poured into your lap"*... God will bring it to us; we don't have to chase after it.

Once again – this is not a "health, wealth and happiness" claim. Blessing from God may not look at all like the packages the world offers. But His blessing has no expiration date, and each of His blessings is accompanied with purpose and fullness.

The world's blessings will always leave us wanting more. This world cannot satisfy; only God can. If we are looking to the world's blessing and approval to satisfy us, we will come up empty every time.

The worldly response leaves us so consumed with looking out for ourselves, afraid of what promoting someone else might do to hurt our own growth, or just too plain busy to notice someone else, that we won't be led to offer encouragement and praise to one another near as often as we should.

The silence can somehow become deafening. We feel frustrated. We feel defeated. In our validation-starved state, we will either be tempted to strive harder to boast in ourselves or will stall out, feeling resentful, defeated and bitter.

We must remain firmly planted in His promises and His purposes. Let's not waste our striving on selfish ambition. We can strive to enter through the narrow door *(Luke 13:24)* or strive to keep the Lord's Day of rest *(Hebrews 4:9-11)*, but let's not strive over anything selfish or shallow.

Rather than striving, let's simply resolve to diligently do what He has called us to do, and trust Him with the results. As I once heard Bianca Othhoff teach, "Response is up to us. Results are up to God."

The P31 woman's response (aka "*her works*" and "*the product of her hands*") are what initiate her praise. Not her own words. Not her selfish wanting. Not her worthless whining.

Her *humble* response of obedience.

Now, let me clear. Our works do not save us. God's Word is clear that salvation is not earned, but is graciously given. *"For it is by grace you have been saved, through faith – and this is not from yourselves, it is the gift of God"* (Ephesians 2:8).

But *"faith without works is dead"* (James 2:17). Our actions back up our beliefs. Despite setbacks. Despite hardships. Despite discouragement.

Let's consider the teaching of Jesus:

> *Beware of false prophets who come disguised as harmless sheep but are really vicious wolves. You can identify them by their fruit, that is, by the way they act. Can you pick grapes from thornbushes, or figs from thistles? A good tree produces good fruit, and a bad tree produces bad fruit. A good tree can't produce bad fruit, and a bad tree can't produce good fruit. So every tree that does not produce good fruit is chopped*

down and thrown into the fire. Yes, just as you can identify a tree by its fruit, so you can identify people by their actions. Luke 7:15-20

In order for God to get the glory, our lives must show that Christ is maximized and others are prioritized. Again, it's not about perfection. But it requires that we consistently force ourselves to examine our own lives:

What is our motive?
Who are we pointing people to?
What's our desired result?

Here's our choice: The way we live our lives will either point others to Christ or point them to ourselves. If we choose the latter, we will always be limited in trying to do things on our own. But our influence is unleashed to being *unlimited* when God is working in us and through us.

Let's not limit ourselves to the blessing we are able to achieve on our own. Let's set ourselves up to be blessed by a blessing that we aren't even capable to imagine.

Now to Him who is able to do immeasurably more than all we ask or imagine, according to His power that is at work within us. Ephesians 3:20

His power. Not ours.

His wisdom. Not ours.

His ability. Not ours.

Bottom line: By choosing humility, we simultaneously choose His strength, which is the only thing that will enable us to embody the character we've studied together over the last 31 days.

We can't do it in ourselves. But praise God that He is willing to do it through us as we submit ourselves fully to Him.

#P31Prayer

God, it's in Your goodness that You don't ask us to live for You in our own ability. Thank you for equipping us in advance for every good work *(Ephesians 2:10)*. We praise You for being alive and active in us. God, help us to exercise humility in our lives. Help our hearts to be more concerned with Your glory. Focus our intentions on blessing others more than receiving blessing. Cease our striving for anything meaningless. Jesus told us that we could learn from Him since He was humble in heart *(Matthew 11:29)*. Don't let our pride get in the way of learning from the amazing example of Your Son. We know that as we humble ourselves, You will lift us up *(James 4:10)* and that Your wisdom follows humility *(Proverbs 11:22)*. Help us to remember that making the choice to be humble is what will seal the deal on our credibility, as we point others to You more than we point others to ourselves. Ground us in gratefulness for all You have done to protect us against our own pride. We know that if we stay close to You, just being in Your presence is enough to keep us in awe of who You are and to face the reality of what our destiny would be without You. God, help us to seek humility, not just in our times of struggle, but also in the days of any success that may come our way. We know that whatever praise we encounter here is because of the results You accomplish through our response. Help us to deflect the glory to You, because we know Your blessing is better than anything this world has to offer. We refuse to sell out to the world and sell ourselves short of Your blessing. We submit everything we are to Your wisdom, Your power, and Your grace. We love you. Amen.

#P31Practice

When I think about everything we've studied over the last 31 days, I know that I am not capable of doing it in my own strength. Not even a little bit.

Jeremiah 17:9 reminds us that our hearts are deceitfully wicked. If we allow ourselves to be the focus of our lives, our routine will inevitably include forsaking God and forgetting others.

Humility not just a principle to live by; it's an action to put into practice.

Humility is a habit.

I'm sure you've heard the story of Jesus washing his disciples' feet. (And even if you know it by heart, I know I'm blessed every time I read it! You can find the story in John 13:1-18.)

But let's take a few minutes to examine just a few of the facts in this story.

> *This event occurs right before Jesus' arrest and death on the cross.*
>
> *The disciples walked everywhere, and their feet were nasty on levels we'll never understand.*
>
> *Washing feet was the servant's job, not the leader's job.*

But as ever with Jesus, there's a powerful lesson in humility here. Even though Jesus was about to pay the ultimate sacrifice for sins He didn't commit, He served and loved sacrificially to the very end. No entitlement. No task beneath him. He realized that a true leader serves sacrificially.

So if we truly want to live humbly, we'll seek out opportunities and find ways to daily "wash someone's feet." Let's open our eyes and hearts and be willing to serve in anyway that gives God glory.

Remember these sweet words from Jesus, *"And since I, your Lord and Teacher, have washed your feet, you ought to wash each other's feet. I have given you an example to follow. Do as I have done to you... Now that you know these things, God will bless you for doing them"* (John 13:13-17).

Humble yourself to serve someone in a way that others in your same position might find beneath them. Maybe some days, you'll humble yourself to go above and beyond to serve your husband, your children, your boss, a co-worker, or someone you supervise.

But maybe God would also have you serve a stranger, a mere acquaintance, someone who can never pay you back or even someone who will not even appreciate the gesture.

None of that matters.

We do it because, in our active obedience, we get to identify deeper with our Savior and gain access to a front-row seat to watch God work.

A few ideas to get your brain churning:

- Commit to asking daily, "Is there anything I can do to help you today?" to at least one person in your household.
- Do someone else's household chore with a smile.
- Plan a special date for your spouse.
- Look for ways to speak encouragement and compliments to others *(especially those who are difficult to deal with!)*
- Give a random gift.
- Make efforts to make others feel like they are the most important person in the world to you in that moment.
- Put your phone down more.
- Prepare dinner for a family who has had a rough season, or invite that family over to your house to join you for dinner.
- Help your children gather toys they no longer play with and donate to your church or local charity.
- Clean out your closet, and donate your clothes to a shelter or non-profit in your city who serves the homeless.
- Help an elderly neighbor or person in your church do yard work or needed household repairs.
- Develop a habit of random acts of kindness. For example, if your child requests a special treat, buy an extra for him/her to give away.
- Put a post-it note on the mirror of a public restroom reminding the next person that they are beautiful and that God loves them.
- Buy some small toys, and deliver them to the children's

wing of a hospital.

- Buy a few extra blankets, and take them to a homeless shelter.
- Drop a note of encouragement in the mail to someone God lays on your heart.
- Visit someone you know who has lost their spouse this year. Never underestimate the gift of your company.
- Pick up trash and throw it away when you see it. It's never beneath us to take care of God's beautiful world.
- Encourage a stranger.
- Pay for the person in front of/behind you in line.
- Ask someone how you can pray for them, and do it right then.
- Mentor/invest in someone else. *(No strings attached.)*
- Do a task within your business that is usually someone else's job.
- Be a good listener.
- Lead by example.
- Give credit away; don't take it.
- Give an extra dose of motivation/encouragement to your co-workers.
- Go out of your way to show your gratitude.
- Offer free baby-sitting for a couple with kids so they can have a date night.
- Cater or cook lunch/breakfast for the teachers at your child's school.
- Buy a few small gifts, and hand them out to your mailman, trash collector, UPS/Fed-Ex carriers, etc. Make sure to attach a note to remind them of God's love.
- Get a few friends together, and tackle a service project for your church – like repainting your pastor's office, pulling weeds, or deep-cleaning the sanctuary.
- Help someone else reach their goal.

My Humility Habits:

after you read

Sweet friend,

I'm humbled you chose to spend the last 30 days with me. I pray God spoke to your heart and that you have a renewed peace and clarity concerning your life's purpose.But there's one thing I have to be certain we are clear on.The P31 woman appears to "have it all." She's growing in her walk with the Lord. She has a thriving marriage. She is a wonderful mother. She has a successful business and ministry.We might find ourselves thinking, "Wow. She has a really *balanced* life. That's what I need: balance."

Oh, sister, please don't fall into that trap. None of us need to live balanced lives.

You see, balanced indicates that everything is of equal importance. And that could not be further from how God has called us to live. He does not desire to be of equal importance to everything else in our lives.

Matthew 6:33 says, *"But seek first the kingdom of God and His righteousness, and all these things will be added to you."*

Balance is not the answer. Surrender is.

Since this goes against everything we typically thought we were looking for, let me say it again:

> ***God doesn't desire for us to live balanced lives that include Him. God desires for us to live fully surrendered lives unto Him, and He'll supply everything else.***

I heard a pastor say once, "When we seek God's best, we'll get the rest."

So that's the truth that makes this possible. To be a true P31 woman, we are not women who have mastered balance, with God as part of our master plan.

Instead, as P31 women, we relentlessly resolve to surrender everything to Him.

> ***He is our Master Plan.***

We must make the conscience decision to live each day with the realization, "I can't, but He can."

Surrender: It has infinitely more power than balance. Let's refuse to settle for mediocre balance.

Let's chase after being fully surrendered to God.

Thanks for racing with me. You encourage my pursuit of Him, and I pray I've had the opportunity to do the same for you.

Let's keep running. Let's daily pick up the pace.

Because this race is the only one that matters.

In Him,
Michelle

notes, quotes & reflections

connect

Connect with Michelle and She Works His Way:

 michellemcnattmyers // sheworksHisway

 michellelmyers // sheworksHisway

myerscrosstraining.com

sheworksHisway.com

Other books by Michelle Myers:

The Look That Kills: An Anorexic's Addiction to Control

Cross Training Devos, Volume One: 21 Daily Devotions

Made in the USA
Middletown, DE
28 October 2017